792.82

D1081027

LABAN FOR ACTORS AND DANCERS

Jean Newlove

LABAN FOR
ACTORS AND DANCERS

*Putting Laban's Movement Theory
into Practice:
a Step-by-Step Guide*

ROUTLEDGE

New York

NICK HERN BOOKS

London

Laban for Actors and Dancers
first published in 1993 in the United Kingdom
Nick Hern Books, 14 Larden Road, London W3 7ST
and in the United States of America by Routledge,
29 West 35 Street, New York, NY 10001
Reprinted 1995, 1998, 1999, 2001, 2007, 2009

Laban for Actors and Dancers
copyright © 1993 by Jean Newlove

Jean Newlove has asserted her right to be identified
as author of this work

Typeset by Country Setting, Woodchurch, Kent TN26 3TB
Printed in Great Britain by Cox & Wyman Ltd,
Cardiff Road, Reading, Berkshire

British Library Cataloguing data for this book is available
from the British Library

ISBN 978 1 85459 160 9 (UK)

Library of Congress data available
ISBN 978 0 87830 044 0

Contents

Sometimes one has great good fortune – the stars are particularly propitious, and were good for me when I met Laban, just as I was leaving school. I had the good fortune to study with him and his colleagues and assistants, Lisa Ullmann and Sylvia Bodmer.

Acknowledgements

To Joan Littlewood, colleague in Theatre Workshop and friend for so long.

To Brenda Okorodudu, who gave of her time so freely whilst I searched for the right words to express my meaning. To Sally Archbutt and Rosemary Cooper, who respectively checked the notation and read. And not least to Nick Hern and Jackie Bodley for patiently guiding me through the mysteries of the publishing world.

Preface

In June 1936 Laban was working as Director of Meister-werkstattin für Tanz in Berlin. He gave a preview of his group dance, *Vom Tauwind und der neuen Freude* (The Warm Wind and the New Joy), which was intended for the Olympic Games celebrations to be held in Berlin the following month. It did not meet with the approval of Dr Goebbels who banned the work after attending the rehearsal. Interviewed by the police about his activities and background, Laban remained under unofficial house arrest over the next fourteen months and officially 'resigned' his directorship. The Nazis banned both his notation and his books; neither was his name to be used in schools.

In poor health and without work or income, he fled to Paris in October of the following year where pupils found him ill and destitute. Laban was brought to England as a guest of Kurt Jooss, who had established a dance school and headquarters for his Ballets Jooss company at Dartington Hall, Devon. His slow recovery to health began.

In 1942, prior to leaving school, I applied for a job advertising a post at Dartington Hall. The trustees wanted someone with dance experience and teaching practice to take charge of the movement training of three hundred women on the estate. I was shortlisted with one other applicant. From my letter, they had the impression that I was in my forties and were rather surprised to see a teenager standing before them. The outcome was better than I could possibly have imagined. They considered me too young for the job and gave it to the other applicant. It appears that after auditioning me, Laban had insisted that I should come and train with him and become his assistant. I met his new partner, F. C. Lawrence, a factory consultant, and was told that I would be introducing Laban-Lawrence Industrial Rhythm to factories and helping Lisa Ullmann (ex-ballet mistress with the Jooss Ballets) to introduce the Art of Movement into the schools.

One of my first jobs after studying with Rudolf Laban was to become the 'movement lady' and choreographer to the

7

original Theatre Workshop Company run by co-founders, Joan Littlewood and Ewan MacColl, who were respectively, producer and playwright, of the company. Both were great admirers of Laban's work and when they heard that he had arrived in Britain and was actually living and working in Manchester, they lost no time in contacting him. As a result of their request for help with the movement training, Laban, whose assistant I now was, sent me along to help out. From then on, I became a regular commuter to Middlesborough, where the company was based. It was to be almost another two years before they moved to Manchester.

Delighted to find a keen bunch of friendly and talented young actors and actresses, I soon decided, with Laban's blessing, to join them full time. Even when the company was rehearsing and performing, the training continued. As well as being their choreographer, I appeared as a dancer in several of the plays. Before long Joan managed to inveigle me into acting roles, simply by telling me that she was one actress short for such and such a play and 'I could do it'!

I was no Sarah Bernhardt and movement remained my first and only consuming passion. Nevertheless, I did act for several years and learned a great deal about actors' problems. I realised how a knowledge of Laban's theories could be of tremendous help in the development of character and behaviour in an actor's training.

In my days at Theatre Workshop, apart from the regular Laban training on a daily basis, actors were encouraged to approach their characters through an exploration of their movement habits and relationships. Voice was always considered as an extension of movement, dialogue came later. Not surprisingly, the company became adept at improvisation.

The results of these training and rehearsal methods won great acclaim, particularly overseas. One highly successful Swedish tour in 1948 ended with the company playing to a packed Royal Opera House in Stockholm. The Swedish and Danish royal families, the Swedish Prime Minister and leading artists from film and theatre were among the audience giving us a standing ovation. The following excerpt appeared in Stockholm's daily newspaper, Svenska Dagblatt the next morning:

Where in Sweden have we a company of actors who can use movement to describe gun-fights, storms, the sea, the tension between people. . . . The speed and suppleness of the actors comes not only from well-trained bodies. It is the result of a dynamic technique of movement. This is the system of Rudolf Laban. The way the actors have their bodies under control helps them concentrate their minds.

My methods have progressed considerably since those early days but they remain absolutely Laban-based and many students have been able to take the work to a fairly advanced level.

From time to time, I have come across misunderstanding concerning Laban's principles of movement, usually from students and teachers whose knowledge is mainly academic. I hope this book will help to overcome some of these problems. It is an attempt to share my own experiences of applying some of Laban's exciting ideas in the world of dance and drama. I hope it will be of practical use to students and inspire others to look more closely at his work. It should be remembered, however, that practical application is the aim. In other words, 'Don't just think . . . MOVE!'

Finally, the art of movement is not something one can learn on a weekend course. It does not end with a recitation of the eight basic 'efforts'. That is only the beginning. Like any worthwhile study, it will take a lifetime. But I can guarantee that the journey will be absorbing and enriching and from early on you will be able to make use of the ideas unfolding before you.

Introduction

'Man moves in order to satisfy a need' (Laban)

Laban looked upon movement as a two way language process through which the human body could communicate by giving and receiving messages. He believed an understanding of this neglected language would lead to a better means of understanding people. First, the student of movement must recognise that all movement stems from an inter-dependence of body, mind and spirit. The child, like early man, had no difficulty in appreciating that movement was life itself (life was one of physical experience).

He agreed that modern man had lost much of this spontaneous joy in expressive movement through his 'reflective delusions' which led to a decrease in tactile ability. The stress was now on the more tangible rewards of work and place in society.

Finally, there were intangible values relating to religion and worship which stressed the spiritual side of his nature.

By observing and analysing movements (which can be conscious or unconscious), it is possible to recognise the need of the mover and to become aware of his inner attitude which precedes the action. This attitude, whether it be a momentary mood or a long-standing personality characteristic, is revealed by the rhythm and shape (or pattern) of the spatial pathway he chooses in a particular situation.

Notation, or kinetography, as Laban called it, helps the observer to get a clear and exact recording of a movement, recalling all the subleties of expression. It is now widely used for recreating dances. For example, *The Green Table*, a ballet by Kurt Jooss, a former pupil of Laban, was first performed in Paris in 1932. It is still in the repertoire, thanks to notation. The notation of modern musicals and ballets is now a matter of course. It has also proved invaluable in industry, sport and therapy as a means of investigating action and behaviour.

It is important to remember that we, as human beings, have a choice of movement and we can change or adapt our movement behaviour at will. A horse can walk, trot, canter, gallop and jump over high obstacles. A cat, on the other hand, is supple and appears to expend little energy. Even in a leap, it appears to remain flexible and relaxed. Stalking its prey, it will watch silently for a considerable time, before pouncing on its victim. At no time would we expect the cat to canter or the horse to pounce. Both animals, like the rest of the animal kingdom, have acquired certain movement qualities over the years which we associate with their particular species. It is, however, possible for us to imitate the movements of the cat and horse or any other animal. Indeed, this often happens in children's games, in Chinese street theatre with its lions and dragons, in the Monkey Kingdom of Chinese Classical Opera and, nearer to home, in Christmas pantomime.

Body movements are the actor's tools; even voice is produced by internal body movements. In order to imitate precisely, the actor must be experienced in observation. It is this attention to detail that makes the artist successful and strikes an inner chord of recognition in the audience. But slavish copying of physical effort is not enough to convey meaning. The actor has to probe beyond this outer shell and search for an inner attitude, whether conscious or unconscious, which is directly linked to the movements observed.

Man may choose to overcome inherited tendencies if he wishes; to acquire good habits even under adverse influences and to control negative behaviour. This ability to select one's movement behaviour is, indeed, fertile ground for the actor or dancer. It enables him to explore many possibilities when searching for his stage character in a given situation. Action and reaction lead to conflict, the dynamic common to all drama, whether it be conflict between protagonists, Man and his Fate or between Man and Society.

It is said that one of the effects of drama is to purge the emotions through pity and fear or through laughter and joy. It is obvious then that drama is largely occupied with the emotions. The audience is able to observe the actor's movements, his pathways through space and their rhythms, and is also affected by the mood they create because of the idea or feeling preceding them. In the following chapters, I will attempt an analytical approach to both the external movement patterns and to the internal attitudes of mind which they express.

Why Laban?

Most aspiring actors today know that it is essential to be able to move well. Their problem lies in selecting the appropiate discipline that will best meet their needs as actors. Classes in tap, jazz and 'modern' dance, yoga, T'ai Chi, meditation, relaxation and the Alexander classes are some of the options usually available.

I would like to make two observations here. First, if you enjoy doing any of these classes, do them. The exercise is good and the fact that you enjoy them promotes well-being. There is also a vast difference between, for instance, learning a specific dance routine and attending meditation and self-awareness classes aiming to improve an actor's own well-being. However, none of these classes will inform you about acting. They will not help you to find the right expressive movement in the elusive search for a character's behaviour in a given situation, nor to develop a technique which will extend your range of movement in the fullest sense. The dance classes with their different styles are only a part of the whole concept of movement. Dance is to movement as poetry is to prose.

In Laban's Art of Movement classes on the other hand, the student is introduced to certain basic movement principles to which all living matter conforms. These laws have always existed but Laban was able to tabulate them and present them in such a way that space was structured and no longer appeared as a 'vacuum'. Once we know WHERE we are going in space, we must observe and analyse HOW we are going and WHAT KIND OF MOVEMENT ENERGY we use. Our choice of the type of muscular energy, or from now on, EFFORT, which determines how we carry out an action, is the result of previously experienced inner impulses. Coupled with our chosen spatial direction it produces a definitive expressive movement quality. Slight changes of effort and/or direction can produce the most subtle differences in expression and meaning. Strongly contrasting movements and directions can radically alter both.

Laban was fascinated by human behaviour and, through his analytical studies, was able to convey to his students a greater understanding and awareness of man's movement patterns. He was equally at home working with opera singers, blacksmiths, actors and engineers.

There are now 'Art of Movement' practitioners in many countries throughout the world: Japan, Israel, Iceland, South

America and Europe to name a few. Their work covers a variety of fields such as education, industry, therapy and the arts.

In the following pages, I introduce the 'Art of Movement' by starting with the most basic exercises as we discover what our bodies are capable of doing and then go on to discuss the three dimensions of movement. This leads us to the Dimensional Scale. In contrast, we discover the qualities of the diagonals and try out the Diagonal Scale. The four elements, Space, Time Weight and Flow are taken separately and then surveyed as a whole. Transitions between the efforts are discussed and the importance of the Time-Weight continuums for Greek drama is touched upon. We go on to explore what happens before any action takes place. Movement clichés in Dance drama are mentioned. Next, I introduce two recognisable mental attitudes and discover how they differ and affect our behaviour. This leads on to a study of complete efforts revealing a great variety of expression in carrying out a simple action. The four drives, the results of earlier studies, are introduced with their components and combinations. The Steps chapter is for all my friends who are terrified of dance routines and finally, I attempt to show how all your studies will help you work on a character whether you are a dancer or an actor.

I would like my reader to see the contents of this book as a journey, a rather remarkable and exciting journey of discovery, during which the traveller will sometimes find the going easy and at other times it will appear tough. But therein lies the challenge of the Art of Movement. I am still travelling along my own movement journey after fifty years and it has remained a constant source of delight, surprise and wonder. I hope a little of this magic will touch all of you in your chosen careers.

Rudolf Laban

(1879-1958)

Laban was born in Poszony in Hungary (now Bratislava in Czechoslovakia). In those days, the whole of south-east Europe formed part of the Austro-Hungarian empire. His father was a high ranking officer and military governor of Bosnia and Herzegovina.

Laban's rather solitary childhood was enlivened by the school holidays when he visited his parents at a fort near Mostar. These visits provided the imaginative and adventurous boy with a wealth of visual excitement as he crossed choppy straits and rode horseback along rugged mountain paths under the protection of an Imam. He enjoyed watching the cavalry as they took part in manoeuvres, marvelling at the intricate designs of their battle strategies. He was intrigued by the folk songs and dances of the regions and was permitted to see a performance by dervishes. He thrilled to see the delicate movement of chamois, the flight of eagles and the extraordinary speed of snakes. On one occasion he was pursued by wolves while skating alone and only just managed to reach the military boat-house and safety. He was interested to see how the local peasantry went about their labours and how the women managed to walk with grace and lightness as they carried heavy loads on their heads.

Working with Laban was like opening a window onto what I had only previously perceived as a distant but beautiful and magnificent view. And now that window was wide open, bombarding my senses, making me aware of colours, sounds, crystalline shapes, spatial pathways, rhythm and harmony. My head was full of the visual splendour and sheer wonderment of it all. I suddenly realised for the first time that I was part of this universal life force.

Laban explained that true dance had lost its way, becoming an artificial art form and a pale reflection of earlier times when it had fulfilled an important role in society. I learned that dance involved one's personality and he made me aware of my own potential as a mover.

I was encouraged to observe and analyse the activity I saw around me – the 'dance of life' as an old lady crossed the road, a stall-holder hawked his wares and a bus conductor whistled to his driver. I was also challenged to try and keep several rhythms going in my head as I listened to the sounds of the street.

He showed me the connection between his movement principles and crystal structures and I learnt about harmony and effort. Seeing I had some modest talent for drawing, he encouraged me and brought out some of his own drawings and cartoons.

I remember with affection the first time he wanted me to try out my art of movement teaching skills. There was no studio at that time, so he volunteered to be my pupil. He stood in front of me listening carefully to what I had to say. He followed the instructions dutifully, if rather awkwardly, as befitting a beginner. However, before long I began to notice his attention wandering and the lesson started to go downhill for me. His movements became perfunctory and he could hardly suppress a yawn. Finally, in some bewilderment I told him, 'You seem to be getting worse.' It seems that after each exercise I had said, 'Good.' As he was so 'good', he saw no reason to try very hard.

He took me to a classical ballet performance on one of our rare free days which I think may have bored him but he wanted to know my reactions, Another time he took me to meet Kurt Jooss and his dance company.

We worked on a new notation for industry together. He was always interested in my ideas and encouraged me to express my views which were always treated seriously. Very soon he was sending me all over the country to give classes and lecture-demonstrations. 'You can do it,' he said.'Of course I can,' I replied with all the confidence of youth.

Laban discussed the letter with me. Could I find the time to take classes at Ormesby Hall near Middlesborough? It seems that a producer had been introduced to Laban's movement scales at drama school. I later learned that Joan had studied 'Modern Dance' in London with Laban-trained Anny Fligg. Unfortunately she had little English and was unable to explain the theory behind her class-work. Joan had also read about his revolutionary work in the German theatre and was determined that her young company should have a Laban movement training. The producer's name was Joan Littlewood and the company was called Theatre Workshop. In the next few years the company's own revolutionary approach to drama was making itself felt both at home and abroad and changing the face of British theatre for ever.

Laban, as always, gave me a completely free hand. By this time I was a fairly seasoned exponent of his work. I believe he also recognised that my real vocation lay in the theatre. My reports back to him made him curious to see the company and so it was, several months later that he met Joan Littlewood and Ewan MacColl, the playwright, for the first time. I took the 'family' as Laban called Lisa Ullmann and me, to see a performance outside Manchester. He was delighted with the production and said that this was the sort of theatre he had attempted in Germany.

When the company finally moved to Manchester, Lisa, who had just opened her Art of Movement Studio, kindly lent the premises to me during the holidays so that the company had good training facilities. Although Laban never took a class for Theatre Workshop, he came to several of our performances, showing great interest in my training methods and my progress as a performer. This continued up to his death in 1958.

I never found any difficulty in understanding Laban although there were times when the language got the better of him. Searching for a word to describe the exact nature of a specific movement often defeated him. (We still have the same problem today!) He would look at me in some exasperation and say, 'Diss t'ing... whatsoever ... you know?'

Chapter 1

Starting Out

If the studio floor is smooth and reasonably clean, all exercising should be practised barefoot. Failing that a soft, flat, acrobatic-type shoe which fits the foot like a glove, is ideal. I do not like the soft ballet shoe which has the upper gathered into the small leather sole. The sole tends to prevent the foot arching and soon comes apart at the seam. Trainers are out, we need to feel the floor under our feet and develop this growing awareness in all our improvisations. Kit should be light, clean and comfortable. A track suit, or equivalent, is good for a quick cover up before or after exercise. It should NOT be kept on throughout a class.

Exploring our Movement Potential
Let us start by taking a quick look at the intricate machine which is going to take us on our exploratory journey. Standing in front of a mirror or a partner, preferably barefoot, we observe with little surprise that we have a right arm and leg and a left arm and leg, situated on either side of our spine. Moving these limbs, we become aware that we can take up asymmetric and symmetric positions.

Concentrating for a moment on the legs, we can improvise ways of locomotion such as lifting and supporting weight, falling, walking, jumping, springing and running. Even leg movements on the spot are able to cover a vast area of space from the waist down. However, although this is their natural zone of activity, trained movers are able to extend their leg movements into the upper zone i.e. above the waist. If this is too difficult for the beginner, there is no need to stand upright. Lying on the floor with the legs raised high above the body, allows the mover to explore the upper zone. In both these exercises the experience is one of moving out of the 'normal' zone.

The spine can stretch and bend, arch, turn and twist, affecting both shoulder and pelvic girdle. The arms can act as a counter-tension in locomotion; when the right leg steps forward, it is necessary for the right arm to swing backward as the left arm moves forward to balance the body. Arm movements can also encompass a vast area of space above the waist although their activity becomes restricted when attempting to reach behind the spine to centre back.

The head can turn or drop sideways or circle. We can feel its weight by dropping the head forward onto the chest, raising it slowly and then dropping it backward and again slowly returning to an upright position.

Hands and feet can bend and stretch, grasp hold of an object and release it. Fingers can open wide and close. Further exploration reveals that every joint describes an arc whilst bending (closing) and stretching (opening). It is possible to complete circles with the head, hands, arms, feet, legs, hips and trunk.

Exercise 1
Facing a partner, let one person lead in a succession of slow exploratory movements ending in clearly defined alternate, symmetric amd asymmetric positions. The opposite partner should try and follow the movements closely and, later, take over the lead. Discuss the difference in sensation between symmetry and asymmetry.

Exercise 2
Individually, experiment with the trunk leading the movement. Without strain, see how far it will turn, twist, bend and stretch. Observe and attempt, if you can, someone else's movement patterns. Let the head participate in this activity.

Exercise 3
This time, keep the legs fairly still and experiment with hands and arms leading the whole body in closing (narrowing) and opening (widening) movements.

Exercise 4
Now use your imagination and experiment for yourself. For instance, letting the legs lead the whole body in inspired ways of locomotion: the trunk rising and falling, a crab-wise gait, scissor jumps, travelling and turning and so on.

Mobility and Attention to Detail
Use your whole body and continue to explore its movement

potential in all directions. Sense the shapes you are describing in space, whether direct or circuitous, small or large; become aware of moments of lightness and strength and of quickness and slowness in execution. The fact that the body naturally moves in arcs is an important point of reference for future movement study.

Further Exploration

Work out a solo movement improvisation based on some of the observations given in this chapter. Take time to make your selection and try to be as accurate in your performance as possible. Show your solo to a partner and see if she can analyse what your body is doing; for example, a gathering (bending in) of right arm, followed by a circling of left leg leading to a twisting of the trunk and ending with a run and jump into a symmetric position. It does not have to be a great work of art! The idea is to:

  i) start the observation and analysis process straight away through observing each other's solo movement,
  ii) see how much you can remember and
  iii) give you confidence in putting into practice what you have learnt in this chapter.

At the end of the class, as you change and relax or get ready to leave, try to maintain this new awareness. How did you put your shoes on? Were you in a dreadful hurry, rushing and fumbling, or efficiently quick and economical in the use of space? On the other hand, perhaps you noticed a colleague moving slowly and in a more reflective manner with a certain amount of precision. Always try to spare part of each day for observing other people's movement patterns.

Reminder

I have made this introductory session brief but I believe it is quite enough to get us started. Already you are probably aware of your own limitations in certain areas. Perhaps your back is stiff or one leg feels stronger in support than the other. Recognising these problems is half-way to solving them, Overcoming them through dedicated training denotes real progress. In all the years of teaching Laban, I have yet to come across students who do not have to work hard at improving some aspect of their movement training. So when you are struggling to do something that your colleague does with apparent ease, remember the time will come when they will be learning from you.

Chapter 2

A Logical Form

Some people move badly. They lack harmony going about their everyday actions and are considered 'clumsy'. Others seem to have a natural, 'in-born' grace. They are a 'joy to watch'. What problems does this cause the would-be performer? Regular clumsy behaviour is a disadvantage; exhausting both physically and mentally. But natural grace can be a disadvantage for someone called upon to play a character lacking co-ordination. Alternatively, an awkward and ungainly student may not initially be able to play a character with exquisite mannerisms. Of course, I have chosen two extremes but they do exist in life. Only a study of Laban's principles of movement will overcome such problems. A purely intellectual understanding of his work will be as nothing without the accompanying hard work of exercise. The two go hand in hand, body and mind as one, fused in a single unity or Gestalt. It is only such a unified approach that will enable performers to extend their range of movement and thereby lessen the danger of being type-cast according to inbuilt personal movement patterns. Fortunately, most of us fall somewhere between the two extremes. Nevertheless, if we are to grow as artists, it is essential that we continue to work at extending our movement capability.

The Kinesphere

Let us now differentiate between space within reach of the body and the more general space surrounding it.

The space within our reach, our 'personal' space, is called the kinesphere. It is like a large personal bubble in which we are able to stretch out in all directions whilst standing in its centre, on one leg. If we move away to another part of the room, our kinesphere will always travel with us. If someone passes by quite closely, it is possible for both kinespheres to overlap momentarily. Anything out of reach is situated in the surrounding 'general' space.

In a lecture hall, the audience will usually sit facing the 'front' of the room. Their focus of attention will be on the speaker. In normal conditions, the audience will face the front and have their backs to the back wall. The right wall will be on their right and the left wall will be on their left. The ceiling will be above them and the floor beneath their feet. These six sides of the room help us towards spatial orientation, representing as they do a dimensional cross.

Let us take the three dimensions of length, breadth and depth as our basic elements of orientation in space. The centre, front and back of our imaginary hall relates to the body's horizontal forward/backward dimension, the side walls to our horizontal left/right sideways dimension, and ceiling and floor to the vertical high/deep dimension. In Laban's terminology, these three dimensions represent the dimensional cross.

Whilst it is not important for the student to go beyond what we attempt in this book regarding spatial study, I think the following is interesting as background information. The comprehensive study of logical spatial forms within the kinesphere and their link to the moving body is called choreutics. Some prefer to call it a study of Space Harmony. Others fear that the word 'harmony' will mislead, appearing to be synonymous with harmonious movement. However, my own preference is for Space Harmony. Natural growth in nature is based on the principle of 'crystalline' structure. I am no scientist but I believe it is obvious that man is an organic part of this wonderful world of molecules, protons, neutrons and atoms, of fluids reacting to tone vibrations, of changes in matter caused by heat and cold as energy moves in a spatial-rhythmic tension within the mass. Our own bodies not only displace space, they also move in space and motion in space exists within us.

In all this movement there is a relatedness. Even transient catastrophic or disturbing (i.e. disharmonious) activity is a natural result of what has gone before. Therefore, for my part, I would consider the study of logical spatial forms and their link to the moving body as a study of Spatial Harmony because of an underlying kinship.

Let me end on a lighter note which is also a practical example of what I have been discussing. A certain well-known producer (who shall be nameless) was giving a lecture on training methods within her company. She had found the audience socially conditioned; they were extremely polite and attentive during the first half of the evening. During the break everyone left the hall for refreshments. This gave her time, with the help of members of the company, to enliven their understanding of the dimensional cross. The chairs were turned to face the back wall and many (with clothes and handbags still attached) were taken from one side of the room to the other.

The audience returned, relaxed and stable, prepared to be passive listeners once again. Like the rest of us, they were conditioned to accept the customary as normal and because of this, they were accustomed to a 'normal' three-dimensional world.

The producer came on to the rostrum as the lights dimmed and the audience panicked as they realised things were not in their logical (i.e. 'right') order any more. In the break, chaos had been created out of order. Emotions were aroused and a lot of hilarious activity ensued before they finally settled down, having restored their chairs and property to a more or less 'normal' dimensional arrangement. From then on, they were a much livelier bunch, participating well in the general discussion.

It seems that we are creatures of habit, conditioned to view the world in a certain way. We expect to face the front when addressed by a speaker, to feel the floor beneath our feet and see the ceiling overhead. The audience knew where they had left their belongings, e.g. to the right or to the left; it was imprinted on their minds. All was safe and ordered until the interval. On their return, nothing was as it had been. The brain was sending out confusing messages. Order had turned to chaos and safety had given way to feelings of insecurity, even anger.

Up-down Dimension

Unlike other animals, our species, through evolution, has chosen to carry itself upright against the force of gravity.

One of our first tasks, as babies, is that of learning to balance in an upright position on two very unsteady legs. With practice, we gradually achieve a perfect vertical posture, directly poised above our point of support. Much later we learn to balance on the balls of the feet (the demi-pointe) and with arms lifted, try and defy the pull of gravity. Such a position is difficult to maintain and one usually returns to the support of the whole foot, which provides a greater sense of stability and with it, an element of security. Continuing our downward journey, as in total relaxation or exhaustion, we sink to the floor giving way to the pull of gravity.

However, movements leading into these directions can never be separated from a parallel inner experience. Reaching skywards, balanced on demi-pointe toes, is often associated with a feeling of high aspirations, with a delicate dream-world of idealistic feeling which seems to overcome, momentarily, our more normal earthbound state. As we leave this transcendental world, slowly descending to a more secure position with our feet slightly apart and gently pressing toward the ground with the soles of our feet and pelvis, knees bent, we acquire a greater stability. There is a readiness within us to deal with any given situation. This preparedness shows a strengthened intention toward action.

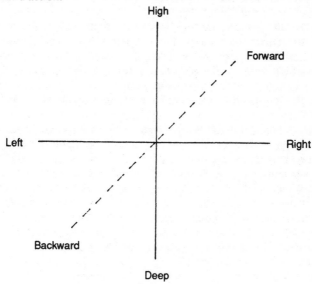

The Dimensional Cross

Left-Right Dimension
This sideways dimension is concerned with inward and outward movements. When we open our arms wide, it seems as if we wish to communicate with someone; our intention is expressed in an expansive outward-reaching movement. Crossing the arms over the chest inhibits communication. It is as if we wished to remain private and keep our thoughts to ourselves.

25

Forward-Backward Dimension

A sudden shock brings a quick reaction backwards, the spine curving as the front of one's body contracts away from danger. When the threat is past, we can slowly advance forward, sustaining a cautious progression.

Exercise 1

(a) With feet slightly apart, weight central and body upright, experiment with inclining forward with the whole body. . . attempting to lean rather like the Tower of Pisa. Don't leave your hips behind. You will soon feel off-balance and need to 'recover your equilibrium' or to put one foot forward to stop yourself from falling over.

(b) Try the exercise leaning backwards, balancing on the heels. This requires an even speedier return to a more stable position.

(c) Leaning to right or left sides, but keeping the whole body straight, calls for the body to transfer its weight from two feet over to one foot, progressing across it to its outside border. (The foot without weight remains in contact with the ground).

(d) These attempts to leave our upright position show the hazards that could befall us! Whilst remaining on the spot and keeping the knees flexible, try moving the body (including the hips) quickly and in sequence, rocking forward, backward, to the left side and right side. When done several times one is completely disorientated. Remember that your feet will be constantly changing weight. The whole world will have taken on a drunken appearance, your universe seems to be in chaos. This outer chaotic world is accompanied by an inner experience of turmoil and disorder, a feeling of not being in control.

Exercise 2

Try Exercises 1(a), (b), (c) and (d) again. This time, however, keep the lower half of the body in a stable, upright position and incline only the top half into the forward-backward, right-side and left-side dimensions. Remember to bend from the waist only. There is, of course, much greater stability here and with it, added security. A feeling of being 'in charge' of a situation. Actors who are lacking in mobility, whether in body or mind, will tend to resort to this type of movement when required to take on a character whose behaviour is almost as chaotic as the movements suggested in Exercise 1. An unwillingness to attempt 'off-centre' experimentation keeps the actor's body firmly anchored.

Exercise 3
Imagine a frightening situation. Instead of recoiling and con-
tracting the stomach muscles, try expressing fright by thrusting
forward with the chest and arching the back. In other words,
doing the opposite of what would come naturally in such circumstances. The expression now is one of shock which has more to
do with surprise or amazement than fear.

Mobility and Attention to Detail
It is important to practise these exercises carefully. They will
help you to extend your range of movement and enable you to
tackle roles which do not depend on your own particular
movement habits. If your back is stiff, you are going to have
problems at first. With all exercise, start gently and build up. I
am not asking you to perform an entrechat-six or a flying leap.
Remember, I am only trying to show you what your body is
capable of doing. You will be surprised at the Rolls-Royce
machine you own.

It is only in the correct execution of the movement that you
can experience its parallel inner feeling. This goes for all the
exercises throughout the book.

Further Exploration
Using Exercise 2, try a stable progression forward, i.e. from the
waist down, whilst leaning backward from the waist up.
(Standard comic policeman?) Change, leaning forward as you
travel backwards. Travelling to the right, lean to the left and
travelling to the left, lean to the right. I find music a great help
here. If you have a partner, take turns to watch each other.
Observation and analysis of the movement is all important. It
leads to greater understanding. Criticise and copy each other's
performance. Change the sequence. There are many
permutations! Increasing the speed lightens the learning process
and releases tension. After all, it should be fun!

Reminder
In this chapter you have been introduced to three basic
dimensions and touched on the feelings accompanying these
directional movements. You have also been given a few ideas on
how to develop the exercises.

Remember, movement behaviour is not just 'physical'. We
move in order to satisfy a need, whether exhorting the gods in a

Greek play or simply blowing our nose while watching television. Nor should discussion of movement lead to intellectual indigestion. Both purely physical and purely intellectual approaches are deadly. Work on your Rolls-Royces and become good movers. Listen to your bodies. Begin to understand the best way to move, and the result will be harmony. Follow the right pathway in space and you will be well on the way to characterisation.

Chapter 3

Introducing the Dimensional Scale

It is important to understand that when Laban was searching for a foundation on which to build his theory of the art of movement, he turned to the cosmic laws, seeing in them a relationship with human movement at every level: mental, physical and spiritual. His choice, recognised after many years as a dancer and dance teacher, was 'based on the inherent laws of natural movement'. He saw in nature the constant growth and decay of matter, the building up and breaking down of mass and the constant motion of fluids. Always the movement patterns of these activities conformed to regular spatial structures, polyhedral forms encased in each other like a nest of Russian dolls. I propose only to use the concept of the cube as an introductory link to Laban's principles of harmony and effort.

In this chapter and the following one, I will introduce you to two movement scales. Look upon the cube as one of a number of 'hatstands' serving to carry our movement hats/scales. The 'hatstand' is not just a convenient framework or tool, it is the meaningful link between human movement and the personality of the mover.

In learning to sing or to play any musical instrument, the student is introduced to 'scales'. These scales provide the necessary foundation for all future musical education. So it is with the study of Laban's movement principles. The three-dimensional cross forms the basis of our 'dimensional scale' and is the equivalent of a musical scale.

Classical ballet students are required to learn the five positions of the feet and arms, the tap student will be introduced to the time steps and when Greek dance was in vogue, the foundation was the 'frieze' line. These are some of the 'scales' relating to different dance styles. To become better actors, we need to learn more about the laws of movement than the styles of dance. It is this study of movement that will help to unlock the doors to expression. As with the other scales, anyone can attempt our basic scale, but not everyone can do it well. It has to be worked at regularly because only when it is done well can the student begin to realise the quality of expression contained within these movement pathways. We are learning a technique which, in time, will become second nature to us.

Finally, to save lengthy descriptive passages of where we shall move in space, I am simultaneously introducing you to a modified notation as you will see from the following diagrams. Look at it carefully for a moment or two and you will see that the signs are part of a 'user-friendly' shorthand system. You will only need signs showing direction and level and before the end of the book, they will be recognised and read with ease. Here they are:

Six Directional Signs

(a) 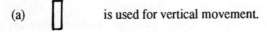 is used for vertical movement.

(b) 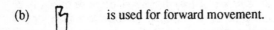 is used for forward movement.

(c) 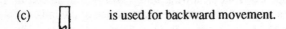 is used for backward movement.

(d) 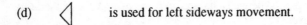 is used for left sideways movement.

(e) 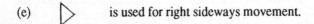 is used for right sideways movement.

However, these signs are incomplete. They do not show the level of the direction. This is done as shown in the diagram at the top of the opposite page.

a) The striped sign shows the high level. (In a step this would mean rising on demi-pointe or the ball of the foot.)
b) The dotted sign shows the medium level (a normal stance.)
c) The blacked-in sign shows the deep level (knees bent.)

30

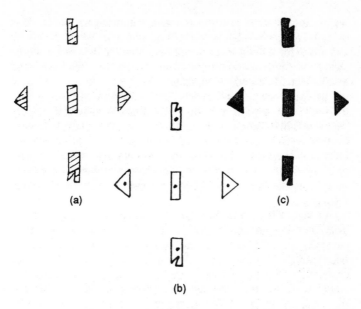

(a)

(b)

(c)

We are now ready to study the Dimensional Scale which, based on natural movement laws, has an affinity with the polyhedral form – in this case, the cube. I have called the cube our 'hatstand'. It links our movement to the personality of the mover.

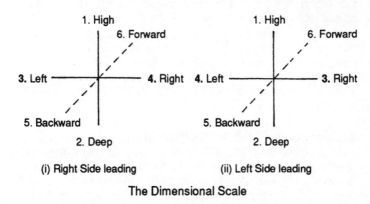

(i) Right Side leading

(ii) Left Side leading

The Dimensional Scale

The dimensional scale, developed from the dimensional cross, gives the mover stability. (Our bodies are constructed in a three-dimensional form.) The supporting leg acts as a pedestal whether we are in a vertical position or leaning into the horizontal. It is essential to reach as far as possible into each of the six directions and work for a fluid interchange of pathways. We will become aware of high, medium and deep levels, of flexibility and freedom in space and its opposite, which leads to a more direct use of space because it is much more restricting to move across the body. The natural reaction of the trunk is to retreat quickly backwards in danger and, when danger is passed, to explore more cautiously forwards. That is not to say that we can only move quickly backwards or slowly forwards. I am discussing a natural reaction. Confronted by a terrifying situation, the body contracts away from the danger and the spine assists by curving to protect the trunk.

As you will have seen from the two diagrams, the vertical dimension is numbered high (1) – deep (2), the sideways dimension (3) and (4) and the backward and forward dimension backward (5) and forward (6). These six directions make up our scale. You will notice I have used two diagrams of the dimensional scale to stress the fact that movement in the sideways direction occurs in a different sequence according to which side of the body is leading the movement. Crossing over the body into a closed or narrow position is taken before the opening out into a wide position. Therefore, if the right side is leading, it will go to its 'closed' left side first (i.e. left 3) and then to its 'open' right side (i.e. right 4.) The opposite is true for the left side. Don't be intimidated by these instructions. Take all the time you need – most of it is commonsense. Remember that the signs relate to a moving body and are guiding you in MOVEMENT through space. Although our cube (hatstand) could be any size, from a pin-head to the size of the earth or beyond, you are concerned with the immediate space within your own kinesphere. Let's now try it out.

The Dimensional Scale for the Right Side
Take a stance position, feet slightly apart and weight evenly distributed. In sequence, we are going to move upward (1) and downward (2), left-side (3) and right-side (4), backward (5) and forward (6). Always remember that the numbering refers to the pathway of the movement and not to its ultimate position.

From stance, I want you to take a very small step forward with the right foot, placing your entire weight on it. As you do this, lead upwards with the right arm until you have it outstretched into the high dimension, your right foot on demi-pointe. The pathway to this position is (1).

Leaving 'high'(1), return by releasing the weight on your forward foot, bringing it slightly backwards to a new position just behind the left foot. Take weight. As you are doing this, lower your right arm and with the weight now completely transferred, lower the whole body to an upright semi-squatting position. Your knee will be bent. The pathway to this position is (2). Return to stance with your arms at your sides. Try (1) and (2) several times.

The right arm and leg are going to move horizontally across the body to the left sideways dimension (3). It is better to turn the right foot out, leading with the heel first. This helps to prevent the body turning to face the direction to which you are travelling. (It keeps the hip back.) The final position of the legs is tightly crossed, bent out-turned knees with the weight on the right foot. As it is out-turned, the feeling is one of sideways balance. Should you have let the feet turn to a normal forward-backward position, the feeling will be different. There will be a forward and backward consciousness. So correct it now. The arm meanwhile has travelled across the chest with the thumb leading, the back of the flat hand resting gently on the far left of the chest. It is an awkward position but has to be mastered. Keep the body vertical even when your knees are bent. The feeling should be one of narrowness and of flatness. Being narrow and flat, the pathway is extremely restricted and therefore, the movement tends to be direct. The left arm moves in counter tension behind the body. The pathway to this position is (3).

Leaving your narrow side (3), move slowly through stance (left foot takes weight momentarily) and continue over to your opposite side. As you take a wide stride out to the right, the right foot takes the complete weight of the body. Simultaneously reaching far out with your right arm, in the same direction, will raise the left foot off the ground. The expressive quality is no longer one of narrowness. There is the feeling of width. In this spatial 'freedom' we have greater movement possibilities than we do on the closed or narrow side. The right knee is out-turned and slightly bent. The raised left leg and right arm have a counter horizontal tension which helps to keep the body from turning to the right. The pathway to this position is (4). Repeat (3) and (4) several times.

Once again, we return to stance and our heels touch fleetingly before the right leg takes weight as it steps into the backward dimension (5). We now encounter a problem. If we take our right arm backwards over its wide or open side, we shall find ourselves turning towards the arm and the movement will once again lead into a sideways dimension. It is better to avoid this by bringing the right arm across the body and backwards underneath the left armpit. This provides counter tension and helps us to maintain our 'front'. The trunk is leaning backward sufficiently for us to have to raise the front (left) leg off the ground. The pathway to this position is (5).

Transferring the weight, we move on to the final position with a step forward. The right leg takes the weight in its new forward position, the right arm moving to an outstretched position in front of the body (6). This forward stretch raises the left leg backwards in a counter tension, leading to a forward-backward horizontal line from right arm forward through to left leg backward. Repeat (5) and (6) several times.

Repeat the Scale – this time lead with the Left Side. Take plenty of time over the scale. Remember to try and keep facing front and then your moves into the various directions will be simple.

Exercise 1
a) The scale can be performed as a series of swings rather like three complete 'figure eights'. In this case, all you do is move in a swinging arc, or curve, from one direction to another instead of moving directly, 'as the crow flies'. The same rules apply as formerly but now you are enjoying the flow of the movement. If music is used, select something which will assist this swinging, harmonious quality. Don't forget to try both sides.

Mobility and Attention to Detail
It is of the utmost importance to persevere with the movement exercises to increase your understanding of the dimensional scale. In the early days, I often came across students who assumed an intellectual knowledge of Laban's work was all that was necessary. No progress was made until they overcame this barrier. Practical ability is the halfway stage in an actor's career and it requires a self-imposed discipline. There are no short cuts. The rewards of practice are when one suddenly realises that one can do something effortlessly which before had presented great difficulty, a wonderful moment that denotes real progress.

Further Exploration

Try moving into the high zone by balancing on the ball of the right foot and then the left. Or take a few running steps and spring into high with one side of the body leading and repeat on the other side. (By this, I mean jumping off one foot and then the other.)Try the springs to each side, (either crossing or opening), or in travelling backwards or forwards. Don't be afraid to improvise.

Experiment with a sideways step to the left with the left foot, followed by a spring off that foot and, making a complete left turn in the air, before arriving at your final position. You could land on both feet for increased stability or live dangerously by landing on the same foot or changing in mid-air to the right foot! The variations are endless. Percussion is often very useful in these experiments.

Using your new awareness, take up your stance position with eyes closed and arms relaxed at your sides. Concentrate on your body. You are going to remember how it felt to travel into the dimensions once again. Making very tiny, barely perceptible movements and not leaving stance, experience inwardly the feeling of rising and falling, the narrowing and widening, the shrinking in retreat and the cautious progress forward as you left the shrinking behind. Be conscious of the polar opposites of each 'end' of the dimensions. Remember, the movement will be very slight, barely noticeable to the observer but you will sense it. Regulate your breathing. It is the very beginning of our personality search.

Improvisation

Do not go straight into the following acting improvisations without working through the preceding exercises.

(a) Keep to the rules of right and left sides of the body leading. Imagine that, in moving into each dimension, you are now taking hold of some object and disposing of it somewhere else. For example, take an object off a shelf in the high zone and leave it on the ground. Snatch another object from the closed (narrow) side and release it on the open (wide) side. Reach backward for a third object and deposit it on an imaginary table in front of you. Try it with the other side leading. Music with an increasing tempo makes for agility and tends to overcome a too profound approach!

(b) Select your own areas, mixing right and left sides of the body as you will. The right arm could go over to its own side and the left leg could cross into the same direction. (Repeated, with a hop or turn, it could develop into a dance routine.) However, our objective is now simply to use what we have learnt in an everyday behavioural situation. So give yourself reasons for all your actions. I know that, as actors, you will be able to build a great fantasy around your performance. A word of warning. Don't get carried away and lose sight of the reasons for doing the improvisation. The main objective is to reinforce what we have learnt.

(d) Add dialogue.

Reminder

Test your observation. Look again at the diagram of the Dimensional Scale on page 31. Give yourself a minute or less to check it out then turn the page over. Remember these signs do not represent a final position. On the contrary, they denote the particular pathway in space along which you are travelling. Stand up and perform the following movements:

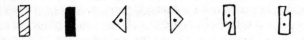

How can you tell which is the leading side? The answer lies in the right/left dimension. Our notation above shows the sideways dimension as left (3) and right (4). The narrow, crossing movement comes first in the scale and therefore, it must be the right side leading. If it were for the left side, it would be as follows:

Chapter 4

The Diagonal Scale

Let us leave the relatively safe shores harbouring the stabilising form of the Dimensional Scale. The hatstand cube has another exciting mystery for us to unravel in the labile (unstable) form of the Diagonal Scale.

As we head for the choppy waters of the open sea, the movement ship tosses and rolls with the swell and we slither and stagger from one side of the deck to the other. Trying desperately to regain our equilibrium, we are continually being thrown off-balance. And yet, despite these difficulties, or because of them, tremendous excitement is generated and the adrenalin flows with the feeling of living dangerously. My favourite scale!

Exploring the labile form of diagonal movements in the studio also gives rise to similar feelings of excitement. The body can only move into a diagonal for a brief moment in time before gravity intervenes and returns us to a stable dimension. However, in that moment we experience a very different emotion from that of moving along more stable pathways. The body is inclined off-centre. This means that we are not in the 'normal' upright, vertical position and are, therefore, off-balance. The most labile diagonals occur in the diagonal scale. These we call 'pure' diagonals as they are equally influenced by all three dimensions. The dimensional scale is stable whereas the diagonal scale is labile.

I would like to remind you that the cube form can be of any size. It is convenient to consider it as filling your personal space, i.e. your own kinesphere. If you are lucky enough to work in a well-proportioned room, it helps to stand in the centre and practise the scale. In your imagination, try to reach beyond the personal space and corners of your cube into the far corners of the room beyond. Remember that the signs refer to the direction of the MOVING body along a diagonal pathway and not to a posture.

You have already learnt the signs for the six dimensions and now we have eight directional signs for the diagonals. This completes our modified notation. It is, however, completely adequate for our needs in this book.

As before, you will see that the striped sign means high level and the blacked-in sign means deep level. Apart from 'centre cube', shown as a vertical dotted sign, there are no other dotted signs. (This sign also shows the approximate centre of the body, i.e. the navel.)

Your movements will take you along each diagonal pathway, always passing through the centre of the cube and travelling from one corner to its opposite corner.

You will not be surprised to see that once again we differentiate between the movements of the right and left sides of the body. In the following diagram, the first movement is to the body's open side. This means that the right arm and leg will move along a diagonal pathway to the right and when the left side leads, the first movement will travel to the open left side.

Let us now study the pathways of the Diagonal Scale for the Right Side and then you will be more informed when carrying out your own dance and acting improvisations.

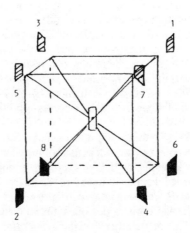

The Diagonal Scale: Right Side

All three dimensions have equal influence and are equally stressed in the movements:

RHF = Right-High-Forward.

LDB = Left-Deep-Backward.

LHF = Left-High-Forward.

RDB = Right-Deep-Backward.

LHB = Left-High-Backward.

RDF = Right-Deep-Forward.

RHB = Right-High-Backward.

LDF = Left-Deep-Forward.

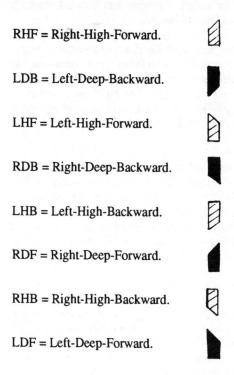

Try to follow the sequence of the scale as given below. Work through it as well as you can. Through trial and error, you will learn a great deal about your body's movement potential. Later, I add a few reminders which you may find helpful. I have tried to keep the instructions to a minimum. Remember this is the Diagonal Scale for the Right Side.

1. From a stance position where both feet are together, supporting the weight of your body, step out with the right foot, the right side moving along a spatial pathway, to the RHF corner. Transfer the weight completely and balance on the demi-pointe if you can. The left leg remains behind, just off the floor. There is a feeling of counter tension throughout the body from the right arm forward to the left foot backward.

Note that it is important to feel the strong influence of three dimensionals all pulling in their different directions simultaneously i.e. high, right sideways and forward. As with all the diagonals, you feel off-balance.

2. The right arm and leg will now travel along a pathway to the LDB corner, the left foot taking weight for a moment as you pass through the centre of the cube to kneel on the right knee which now takes over the weight. The right arm crosses in front of the body, giving it a strong twist against the right knee. The head and trunk incline towards LDB. You will feel off-balance.

3. The right arm and leg lead the body through the calm equilibrium of the vertical centre before travelling along another pathway to LHF. The right foot takes over the weight on demi-pointe. (Make sure to keep your body facing the front of the room.)As the right foot has crossed to the left side, it leaves the left foot on the right, behind and just off the ground. The effect is of a strong counter twist throughout the whole body.

4. The right arm and leg travel (via centre) along an opening diagonal pathway to RDB. Reaching into the corner, weight on the right foot, knee well bent, the counter tension is felt strongly, particularly if the left leg is raised to a high level. Sometimes this movement is taken in a kneeling position. I prefer to use the former movement.

5. The body recovers its equilibrium momentarily as the right arm and leg lead a movement returning through stance. This newly regained equilibrium is soon relinquished as the movement continues, crossing over to the LHB corner. The right foot having crossed over (behind the left leg) to the left, takes weight on the demi-pointe. The left knee is slightly bent across the front of the right leg and the left foot points towards the RDF corner. The right arm crosses in front of the body reaching towards LHB. The feeling of twist and of being almost off balance is noticeable.

6. Your diagonal pathway now travels to the RDF corner via 'centre'. The right knee is bent and the right arm reaches into

the corner of the cube and beyond. The left leg is raised high in counter tension in a LHB direction. The body feels the open stretch and pull of the three dimensions – right, deep and forward.

7. Passing 'centre', your right arm and leg move into the RHB corner of the cube. The body arches as it follows the movement. Balance, as in all the corners of the cube, is precariously maintained and the inter-tension of the three dimensions is strongly felt.

8. This diagonal takes you along your final pathway to the LDF corner. The right arm and leg lead the way, crossing over stance and as you 'pierce' the corner the familiar feeling of twist is experienced. The left arm and leg provide counter balance in the RHB direction. (Remember to 'keep your front', i.e. face the same direction as when you first started the exercise.) Return to stance, i.e. original, upright, vertical position, weight on both feet. Repeat the Diagonal Scale for the Left Side:

| LHF | RDB | RHF | LDB | RHB | LDF | LHB | RDF |

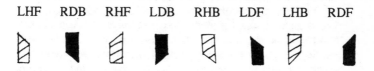

Note

I have tried not to weary you with pages of instructions. As a result, your attempts to perform the diagonal pathways may not be very precise. Like learning to sing or play a scale in music, there will be several wrong notes in the early days of your training. It doesn't matter. You will be learning about the quality of expression contained within these spatial pathways and how they affect your body. I believe it is more important at this stage to recall the 'movement ship in choppy seas' and the exhilarating experience of momentarily defying gravity by leaning off balance. (i.e. labile movements as opposed to the more usual stable movements in our everyday life.).

The following exercises will help to reinforce your understanding of the labile quality of the diagonals. They are based on

41

working actions and very simple dance movements. Although all the exercises should be worked through eventually, I would suggest concentrating on one 'wall' at a time.

1(a) Find a space and turn around with your arms outstretched. Make sure your kinesphere does not overlap into anyone else's space. Now shut your eyes and imagine the cube has become a bare room taking up all your personal space. Its front wall consists of one huge window which badly needs washing! Stand in the centre of this room with your feet together, weight evenly distributed. Face the front. You will only use the right side to lead the washing operation and only wash the right side of the window. It is vitally important to pay particular attention to the corners. The high corner will bring you up onto the toes of the right foot; washing the deep corner of the window will result in a deep bend of the right knee. The counter tension will result in the opposite side of the body inclining towards the opposite end of the diagonal. (If you are really flexible, the left leg may even reach into the high zone in the backward dimension!) Be very aware of the three-dimensional pull as you move into these directions.

(b) You can congratulate yourself on having done a good job but it is not quite finished. You now have to wash the left hand side of the window. Try doing this with the left side leading. The corners are especially important. Remember to reach far out into your kinesphere. (Your window is not conveniently situated so that you can remain in a comfortable stance position on two feet.) You need to feel off balance at moments and consciously experience the counter tension of three dimensions all having equal influence.

(c) Try repeating the two actions but this time the right side of the body washes the left side of the window and vice versa.

2 (a) Back to the home decorating of our bare room. The left wall has been papered but many air bubbles remain and need smoothing out. Once again I would like you to lead the smoothing operation with the right side. This means that ALL your diagonal movements into ALL four corners will be crossed.

(b) A final smoothing with the left side leading, means travelling now into four open diagonals. Make sure that your wall is sufficiently far away from centre so that the body can feel momentarily off balance.

3 (a) The room is looking much better. Now smooth out the bubbles on the right wall with the right side leading. Follow the previous guidelines.
(b) Left side leads.

4. Use music or percussion.

(a) Face a partner.

A. Right side leading.

B. Left side leading.

(b) Make up your own diagonal exercises with a partner either moving simultaneously or in a flowing succession which can be repeated. It helps to show your work to others, feed-back is useful.

5. With or without music/percussion. Freely explore every surface of your imaginary room. For example, you could touch the ceiling with your right hand, the back wall with your right foot and the right wall with your left hand. Lying on the floor of your room, reach to the higher zone, i.e. the ceiling, with both legs. Continue to lead with the legs moving over all six surfaces. Use *all* the corners.

Mobility and Attention to Detail
(i) Centre cube relates to the centre of your kinesphere and approximately to your body centre, i.e. the navel.
(ii) 'Stance' is where one or both legs, supporting the weight of the body, rest on the ground.
(iii) Pathways travelling from the centre of the cube involving the whole body (as in the diagonal movement sequence we have just performed), increase the body's disequilibrium until they

reach maximum effect at each corner. The Diagonal Scale contains diagonals which pass through the centre of the cube to their opposite corners; we call these 'pure' diagonals as all three dimensions have equal influence. The strongest counter tension (pull in the opposite direction) is needed at the corners if we are not to collapse. However, it should not be too strong to detract from the feeling of momentarily being off-balance.

(iv) When a movement crosses diagonally over the body to its narrow or closed side (as in right arm and leg crossing to the left side), it results in a twisting of the trunk. Remember to keep facing the front of the room. It is very easy to turn the body in the direction of the twist, losing the quality of the movement.

(v) In LDB, the kneeling position should assist the trunk to arch and twist as the right arm, leading across the front of the body, reaches into the corner.

(vi) The signs in the notation are all concerned with the direction of a movement and not a final posture.

Further Exploration

(i) You have a nightmare of being imprisoned in a room. To your horror, it begins to shrink. In desperation, you fight against all six surfaces. The whole body is less able to stretch but has greater flexibility: turning, twisting and rolling. Eventually, the space becomes too small and you are trapped. The only movement left to you is breathing.

(ii) Your prison starts to expand, becoming as large as the entire room. The whole body is released and expresses its new found freedom by moving joyously: stretching, leaping, running, turning, twisting and rolling in a variety of ingenious ways. The feeling of being imprisoned in a shrinking room-like cube is lost in infinity.

Improvisation

(i) Two students meet to discuss a performance they have just seen. One of them carries himself very much in an upright position. There is stability in his movement behaviour. The other one moves in a more dynamic manner. His trunk is rarely seen in the vertical position. Indeed, he seems to enjoy the instability of being slightly off balance and defying gravity. What is the impression these two characters make on observers ?

(ii) Imagine you are trying to walk on the deck of a ship which is experiencing a heavy swell.

(iii) You are in an overcrowded hall and there is no air conditioning. You begin to feel faint and try to make for the exit.

(iv) You have been at a party and although you are not very drunk, your legs are not quite under control.

(v) You are light-headed from lack of food.

Reminder
The Eight Diagonals

RHF – LDB – RHF	LHB – RDF – LHB
LHF – RDB – LHF	RHB – LDF – RHB

I have introduced you to the concept of a cube within your personal space. You have explored the 'pure' diagonals going through centre to their opposite corners. Wherever you turn to face in the room, these diagonals remain constant, i.e. RHF and LHF will always remain RHF and LHF. Your personal space containing the cube rotates with you. However, in the general space outside your own kinesphere, the diagonals remain constant.

I took my dance group to Moscow many years ago. The finale of our dance programme was very exciting. The dancers started off by facing the audience and dancing in unison along 'pure' diagonals. As the music got faster, the dancers started to turn: a variety of quarter or half turns with steps and gestures leading along the diagonals of their own cubes, in their own kinespheres. The diagonals belonging to the general space of stage, auditorium and audience remained constant. In the excitement of the twirling action, we were aware of the outer unchanging structure of the auditorium which helped our orientation.

Chapter 5

The Flow of Movement

A continuous and uninterrupted sequence of movement is said to have a 'flowing on' quality. In contrast, when the sequence is broken by movements which stop and start, the 'flowing on', or continuity, has been replaced by jerkiness.

The flow is successive when the movement passes from one adjacent body part to another. It is simultaneous when the whole body is engaged in moving at the same time.

It is possible to move in a continuous, flowing and successive way. A trunk movement can, for example, travel upwards from the knees, through the hips, chest, shoulders and head. These movements are often curved or undulating, i.e. relating to the arcs and circles mentioned in our previous studies. For successive flow, the movement of the adjacent parts of the arm and leg would be shoulder, elbow, wrist, hand (fingers) and their reverse order or hip, knee, foot and their reverse order. It is not possible to move successively in a backward direction with the hip, knee and foot because the knee only bends forward.

One can also move successively in an interrupted, jerky manner. An example would be that of a series of 'staccato' movements from shoulder to elbow, wrist and hand.

Simultaneous flow of the body can also be continuous or jerky.

Exercise 1

Move for your own pleasure in a tranquil manner, neither too slow nor too hurried. Concentrate on the flowing continuity of your improvised movement sequence. Avoid moments of awkwardness, of sudden lack of concentration or pausing in order to come to terms with a difficult position. If you are in a class, watch the other students. Observe the more successful 'performers' in this exercise; discover, through analysing their movements, what makes them appear at ease with continuity. Try it out for yourself. Partners in all these exercises can be very helpful, explaining and showing moments when the continuous flow seems to falter. Try and relate these specific jerky periods to the precise moment of their happening.

Exercise 2
Try an interrupted, jerky, discontinuous, movement sequence. Avoid the tendency to increase the speed at this stage.

Exercise 3
(i) Experiment with successive body movements. Here is an example using the whole body: Stance, arms held high above the head. Start with the fingers curling downward followed by wrists and elbows. As the flow reaches the upper arm, the head is lowered and the shoulder girdle leans forward followed by chest, hips and knees sinking to the floor. Return to the vertical position in the same order or in reverse order, starting with the knees moving upwards. In this example the body is symmetrical.
(ii) Stance. Raise the right knee, right hip, right shoulder, right elbow, right hand. Return to stance and repeat with the left side.

Exercise 4
Stance. Arms high above the head. The whole body drops simultaneously, 'like a stone', to a crouched position, pauses, and returns simultaneously to its starting position.

Exercise 5
Try mono-linear movement (a direct line between two points) in a continuous sequence. Because the movement passes from one adjacent part of the body to another, there will be a feeling of 'flowing on'.

Exercise 6
Let the movement flow through the body successively but with interruptions, i.e. in a jerky or 'broken' manner. A simple example would be moving from shoulder, elbow, wrist to hand (fingers) in four separate successive actions or, perhaps, hip, knee to foot in three separate successive actions.

Exercise 7
Try a poly-linear pattern (several directions overlapping, multi-

dimensional) with simultaneous movement, i.e. when all the body parts are active at the same time. Simultaneous movements can either be continuous or interrupted.

Improvisation
Exercise 1
(i) Try a variety of ways of locomotion: turning, rolling over the floor, walking forward, running sideways, crawling backwards while reciting a well-known nursery rhyme. Try repeating the movement sequence exactly many times. A more advanced activity would involve the use of chairs, rostra and steps. New ways of surmounting these obstacles should be tried. With an experienced company, I was able to use the sets on the stage with its attendant difficulties of a steep rake.
(ii) The exercise should now be tried with a speech or poem that is in the process of being learnt.
(iii) Observe other students' movements for variety. See how the voice accompanies the activity whilst reciting the well-known rhyme.
(iv) What happens to movement and voice when the speech is less well-known? Remember voice is an extension of movement.
(v) Now try some of the early exercises (1-7) with voice, either with rhymes or a description of what you are doing as you move, i.e. with a running commentary.

Bound Flow
Flow is considered to be bound when an action can be stopped at any given moment. This will not be a complete stoppage leading to an abandonment of the action, but a pause. Although the movement has stopped its spatial journey, the sensation of fluency remains during the pause but is, however, controlled to the utmost. Such pauses in action can occur for a variety of reasons: sensing an error, needing to adjust or to correct, a change of mind or any other need to put the action 'on hold'. It is a cautious approach.

Free Flow
Flow can be considered to be free when it is difficult to stop suddenly. The mover feels there are no problems. He is not expecting errors, a need to adjust or to change his mind. Confident, he sees no reason to put the action 'on hold'. There is

a 'whole-heartedness' about this fluency of action. It is a confident approach.

Not all actions are cautious or confident. One can perform a routine task taking appropriate action at every stage. In this case, one does not expect to alter the movement because of problems and neither does one take a confident, whole-hearted, approach to the task. The emotions do not, in this instance, play a dominant role.

If you were working at a new job using dangerous machinery, it would be sensible to use all necessary caution. If the working actions followed each other on a regular, unchanging basis, you might eventually treat the whole job as routine. I wonder if it would ever become free flow? Very much would depend on your suitability for the job. Supposing, however, parts of the action were constantly changing so that you could never take any stage for granted. Free flow would surely be a wrong choice because of the danger at any time. And yet, there might be some very gifted operator who had such expertise that he could use it with success.

On the other hand, I think we have all experienced the sight of people moving with the utmost caution over the simplest of tasks and seen foolhardy types moving whole-heartedly to help in a situation requiring far more cautious consideration. Observers are often reduced to frustration or hilarity by this incongruity of behaviour.

Look back at the improvisation section in this chapter. Do you remember your first efforts at locomotion; the caution and the breaks in continuity with which you approached your early 'trial runs'? After much perseverance, you probably mastered the complicated route you had planned. It began to lose its novelty and you, your fears. The words began to come without difficulty. The whole exercise became routine.

I wonder if you moved into the free flow and confident stage? Did you find something along the route and/or certain words which lifted you out of the 'routine' state? Did something excite you, set the adrenalin working overtime? Using any degree along the bound/free flow continuum to express your emotions, you might have crawled or somersaulted into enjoyable fury, despair, sorrow, delight, hilarity or tranquillity.

Exercise 1
Repeat the earlier exercises with all this in mind, choosing a new route. Observe and analyse each others' movements. Difficulties

49

should not end up in long discussions but any advice proffered by the observer should be followed up by a demonstration. This is good practice as it also extends one's own movement range. The flow experience will be variable and depend upon your practical ability and degree and type of commitment to the movement. Don't worry over the time taken. It really doesn't matter. I am only concerned that you should:

(i) understand what we are trying to do,
(ii) experience the sensation and feeling for yourself,
(iii) recognise it in your partner's performance.

Exercise 2

You all know the children's game, O'Grady says 'Do this' and 'Do that'. Everyone takes up positions on the command, 'O'Grady says, 'Do this''. When the caller only says 'Do that', the idea is not to move, keeping the previous position, or you are out of the game. This is a light-hearted exercise but I have seen some extraordinary developments. Those who move mistakenly on 'Do That', must go into a character they have played or studied in some depth. Failing that, a well-known poem or nursery rhyme would do. At first, they hold the position and then use it as a basis for their character as the speech progresses. The position often includes facial contortions. I have seen a grotesque Desdemona and an ethereal Sir Toby. Strangely enough, this exercise has been found to assist in the search for characterisation. We will explore this later.

Mobility and Attention to Detail

Concentration is often greatly assisted by closing the eyes in the early stages of sensing continuous, discontinuous, successive or simultaneous flow and their permutations. With practice, your awareness of flow will be heightened. However, there will be transitional moments, moving from one strand of the flow thread to another, which are difficult to analyse. Don't worry. It is more important to:

(i) go for the main action(s).
(ii) become aware of the body's inner preparation prior to the transitional change. Did certain muscles tighten up, or relax, in response to the messages they received? In other words, how do they prepare for change?

Further Exploration

With all the above exercises conscientiously worked through, it is now time to pay attention to breathing. Discover what natural changes occur as you move from one strand of flow to another. Although you are concentrating on your breathing now, if you are to receive the correct information, you must perform the movements to the best of your ability.

Chapter 6

Space

*Our bodies displace space, move in space, and
motion in space exists within us.*

Lie with your back on the floor, arms by your sides and knees
bent. The soles of the feet should be slightly apart. Feel the floor
beneath the feet. (This position is also used in voice classes.)
Feeling quite relaxed, try and 'tune in' quietly to the activity of
your own body. The sensation should be one of ease, of a gentle
focus on what is happening within. Relaxation does not mean
floppiness or heaviness but rather a light tension – a 'bodily
awareness'.

Certainly you will 'know' intellectually that the heart is
pumping and the blood circulating. If you come to this exercise
after some strenuous activity, you will feel the heart's pounding.
If you are completely rested, it is likely that you will feel nothing
at all of its non-stop rhythm. Commonsense tells you that it is
going on regardless.

Now bring the knees onto the chest, curling your toes
underneath. Bend the elbows and thrust them tightly into your
sides, clenching your fists. Exhaling, try and squeeze all the air
out of your body. The head will disappear into the shoulders.
Increase the tension and squeeze hard for a count of twenty. Let
go, relaxing into your former light tension and allow your
breathing to return to normal.

Repeat the exercise but this time lift the head and shoulders
onto the knees and try and occupy as little space as possible by
squeezing up into a tight ball. Have someone count twenty and
return once again to your original position with the feet on the
floor. Tune into your breathing. Feel the strain leaving the body
as it relaxes from its cramped position and the breathing returns
to normal.

Inhaling fully, we can fill our lungs with air and hold our
breath for some time, trying to take up more of the surrounding

space. Exhaling fully, we can expel all this imprisoned air and try keeping it out; making ourselves smaller. Sooner or later, we are compelled to take in more air. We can try and squeeze our life blood out of our bodies but the Rolls Royce engine soon takes over, order is restored and the blood again circulates freely. The motions of the organs of the body continue with their many functions. And wherever we are in space, however little space we try to use or however much we try to encompass, whether we are active or still, we displace space.

Now let us turn our attention to the kinesphere surrounding us. How do we use space? At one polar end of the spatial continuum, our movements are direct and linear. At the other end, they are flexible and plastic. Midway along the continuum, they follow the natural movement curves and arcs normally used in everyday actions, being neither overly direct nor excessively flexible but mid-way between the two.

A direct movement can be likened to an arrow travelling straight to its target. Attention is on the point of arrival, the use of space is economical and restricted.

A flexible movement, curving, roundabout and plastic, allows us time to look around the spatial garden and smell the flowers.

The outward journey of any movement, i.e. from the trunk to the periphery, is said to be centrally guided. I always think of the navel as the body's centre. The return journey, from the outer kinesphere to the navel, led by the hands and/or feet is said to be a peripherally led movement. With the limbs closer to the body, it is possible to indulge in much greater flexibility, centrally led. The more the limbs spread out into space, the greater their directness. Flexibility gives way to peripherally led movements.

Exercise 1
(i) Stance. Stand in front of a partner, sufficiently close for you both to be able to reach out and touch each other, arms held loosely by your sides. Shake hands and return to the original position. Try to remember your action and repeat it exactly. Do this several times. Analyse your own movements. It may help initially, to close your eyes and try to sense the moment your body mobilises in response to the message received, immediately prior to the action. Is the action centrally guided? Does the arm describe an arc as it moves into the forward dimension? Was your movement continuous or jerky, simultaneous or successive, bound or free flowing? Most probably

53

it was performed as a routine exercise; after all, you must have shaken hands many times over the years. It has become an everyday 'working action'.

Look at other people shaking hands. Does their action differ in any respect? If so, how? What is different about their movement? Back up your theory with a demonstration. This means, of course, not only going through the motions but trying to get to grips with the feeling, the mood, preceding the action.

You will find that you have, by now, accumulated quite a vocabulary to describe movement in general terms. And, hopefully, you are looking around with new eyes, able to discern nuances of expression that escaped you earlier.

(ii) Try a variety of handshakes in different dimensions. This is best attempted within a tightly-knit group, facing different ways. Small people could reach upwards to their taller colleagues to shake hands. Explore the possibility of shaking hands in the sideways dimension (flexible or direct). Shake a hand behind you whilst the other hand simultaneously shakes hands with someone in front of you. Try not to turn the body too much or the exercise loses its point.

It is possible to improvise a short sequence of handshaking which can be repeated. Music, in this case, helps to synchronise everyone's movements. I imagine that the routine image has been lost, temporarily at least. After all, it is most unusual to shake hands in all these different areas of the dimensional scale. It is not quite 'normal'. It is 'normal' to turn the body to face the person one is greeting socially. We are conditioned to accept the customary as 'normal' in our three-dimensional world. Remember the audience and their confusion.

As artists, we are used to calling upon our imagination. We thrive on it, although sometimes it can be an indulgence and there is a tendency to go 'over the top'. The above exercise will in some cases, I am quite sure, have led to such behaviour. All I would say is that, if you apply the training with understanding, the results will be infinitely superior and more satisfying because you are working at extending your movement range. There will be greater shades of expression along a continuum from depression to elation. The movement and the feeling will be a unified whole.

(iii) This exercise can be done singly, in couples or with a group of students. Success depends on the individual's action, re-action and inter-action with the group. Sounds or gibberish accompany the movements but there is no intelligible conversation.

Stance. Take up any position you like. It can be twisted, curved, symmetrical, asymmetrical, closed, open, crouching backward, reaching forward; high, medium, low (perhaps, lying on the floor); on the toes (demi-pointe) or hands! These are only a few of the choices. The face is also involved.

Start 'locomoting' towards other members of the group accompanied by your voice emitting metrical or rhythmic sounds. Now try excitingly different ways of shaking 'hands', of grasping and releasing. Your hand could reach through your legs to shake the foot of another 'creature' momentarily lying in the foetal position. I'm sure you have the idea. Now take it away.

Mobility and Attention to Detail

Continue to work hard on the body. Having worked through one chapter, do not leave it for ever but go back and repeat the exercises. Continue to improve on your mobility. Sweat! Anyone can learn the theory. The real craft is putting it all into action meaningfully and you can have a lot of fun doing so.

All the exercises have purpose. With improvisation, there is freedom to explore and a much greater opportunity for individual creativity. Do not try for characterisation just yet. The 'monsters' that appear (as in the last exercise), are summoned up out of a vivid imagination based on some knowledge of movement principles. They are ephemeral but they will have enriched your movement potential and the experience will be stored for future use.

Further Exploration

Make up your own exercises based on the work in this chapter. For example, a table set for a meal; helping yourself, helping others, eating and drinking. Observe and analyse the 'performance' of others. Observers can discuss the improvisation using our new-found movement vocabulary. Eventually, take the action away emotively, i.e. with feeling. Introduce voice if you have not done so already. Sounds, gibberish, speech or a mixture of all three. It could be that observers are keenly motivated to join in. Go ahead.

Continuing on this theme, leave the 'routine' table situation and imagine the table fills the whole room. Allow your imagination to take over. Perhaps spin and leap to the teapot, dance with it to wherever the cup is placed. Perhaps you'll fly directly like one of Robin Hood's arrows. Or would you prefer to 'smell the flowers'? Throw or bounce the cup to someone else. These are just a few ideas to get you started. Remember, we are more concerned with movement than witty dialogue.

The teapot and cup will have little significance now as real objects. The hands and fingers will be seen clasping/gripping and releasing/letting go of something. Such versatility in expressive movement, needs practice, not theory. It is only the half-way stage but, nevertheless, it is vitally important to reach this stage. After that, you can perform your movement sequence with real feeling, real expression. Teapots and cups forgotten, the sequence could become 'pure' dance. What will be most noticeable is the fact that you are not 'lost' in space, you are beginning to be in command of your kinesphere.

Reminder
When did you last take time to analyse people's behaviour out-of-doors? Watch their movements at a football match, a fairground, a street market.

Chapter 7

Time

I was a young teenager when Laban introduced me to a whole new concept of time. Stories of the accelerated whirling of dervishes, the measures used by the Greeks in their dramas, the importance of the seasons in the life of primitive man and the inter-relationship of planets and the molecular world led to Time and Rhythm becoming magical words for me. I went away from that first session walking on air. Now the time has come for me to try and pass on some of my own excitement.

To older generations, it seems that life today, in the Western world, is lived at breakneck speed. For instance, modern transport allows us to travel further and faster than ever before. Planes take us across continents with different time zones and cars, trains, buses and helicopters allow us to consider working many miles from home. The bicycle and horse and cart play only a minor role. Walking seems almost to have been relegated to a weekend hobby.

In earlier times, daily life was governed by the seasons. With Spring came the earth's awakening and the planting, with Summer the ripening and in the Autumn came the harvesting. The days had already begun to shorten by the time the produce was safely gathered. The year's growth died back with the first frosts of winter and only a few hours of daylight remained for dealing with daily chores as the old year died. Hope was reborn in the New Year. The earth threw off its wintry yoke with the rising sap and planting started once more.

Our own daily lives are no longer governed by the seasons. Whatever the weather, be it light or dark, we have our own time for rising, going to work, for retiring. We can lighten the hours of darkness; even football is played under floodlights now. Our time is measured in seconds, minutes and hours as well as days, weeks, months and years. The mathematical precision of the twenty-four hour clock is essential to our daily lives. Without it, we would find it very difficult to measure the duration of time accurately. Could we say, with any certainty, the time is now seven thirty-three and five seconds precisely? We are not talking clocks. If we were, we would be automatons and never need an alarm call. Some people pride themselves on this ability but they are the exception to the rule.

A parallel is to be found in music. Time here is measured metrically, as in crotchets, quavers, semi-quavers, minims and so on. These units of time vary in duration one from the other but their values remain constant. As children we were introduced to clapping out a regular beat or walking 'in time' to these units. We call this metrical rhythm.

Our own inbuilt clocks vary tremendously. Shown a list of tasks to be accomplished in a given time and assuming that the workers are equally motivated, one person may accomplish the work easily and still have time to spare. Another may take much longer to tackle only a few of the tasks within the time limit.

A movement not bound by exact metricality is said to have a free, irregular time-rhythm, often leading to more expressive, dynamic interpretation. Of course, there are occasions when one must move expressively to music, particularly in the case of dance. The legs and feet may prefer to follow the music's metricality but the upper body and limbs are free to follow an irregular time-rhythm. Ideally, the performer should, through the body, be able to express the qualities of both regular (metric) and irregular (free) time-rhythms. Free verse is an example of irregular time-rhythm. When talking of duration of time, the continuum is from very short to very long.

We use the word 'motion' rather than 'movement' when talking of inanimate objects. The motion of a falling stone (or Newton's apple) will obey the laws of gravity; the acceleration of the speed of its fall and its path in space always remain constant and can be calculated. The falling objects do nothing to avoid their fall whereas a person falling into a bonfire would surely try to avoid the flames.

The speed with which a movement travels spatially is on a continuum from very fast to very slow. We need to remember that whereas the speed of motion of inanimate objects is constant and calculable, everyday human movements are neither. We are not mechanical. The speed with which we move to accomplish a purpose will tend to accelerate and decelerate depending on cirmcumstance, making for a freer, irregular rhythm guided by our kinesthetic sense. The resulting dynamic qualities lead us to our continuum of *suddenness* and *sustainment*. This we shall use as our basic time continuum, without losing touch with duration and speed.

Do not rush the following exercises.

Exercise 1

This exercise, for two or more students, needs height, a stopwatch and a light object such as a table-tennis ball. There are two objectives to the exercise, namely, (a) to heighten one's awareness of the duration of time, and (b) to improve one's sense of metrical rhythm.

On a command, 'GO', the ball is dropped from a high point and its fall is timed by the stopwatch as accurately as possible – a bare second or two. The rest of the group try to clap in a quick metrical rhythm, quietly counting the number of beats. We know that the object's motion will be predictable, always falling from the same height, it will always travel at the same speed. (I have found dropping the object over a flight of steps or from a first floor window adequate!)

It is more than likely that the partner with the stopwatch will get different readings at first. His own dynamic movement could well be a hindrance until he gains greater control of the experiment.

The clapping group may also experience degrees of mayhem, clapping against each other and with different beats each time. When the experiment is more controlled and practice leads to a clearer sense of metricality, the number of beats should remain the same for any one person. (Some may be using units of longer or shorter duration.)

Exercise 2

This exercise can only be attempted once with a class. Half the group stands in a long line down one side of the room facing across to the other side. They must have a little space on either side of them and all 'toe the line'. The rest of the class are observers. Sometimes it helps to give them a partner whose 'performance' is later observed and discussed in detail. The idea is to walk directly forward, as slowly as you can, and to keep moving all the time. There must be no pauses, hesitations or indirect gestures leading to the step forward. In other words – no cheating! The eyes are shut tight. The mover concentrates on slowness, a constant progression in a forward direction only. The line moves on the word, 'Go'. When some of the faster participants have nearly reached the far wall, the command, 'Stop', should halt them in their tracks immediately. The result usually reflects an amazing variety of degrees of slowness. The winners are, of course, those who have moved continuously in a direct line but covered very little ground. Degrees of fast and slow are shown to vary considerably amongst the participants along the time continuum.

Exercise 3

For students who sometimes find a sense of timing difficult, being either over-hasty or exceptionally slow in daily life, this exercise could be of use.

Two partners are required. B uses the stopwatch to control the experiment. The moving partner A, stands quietly still in stance. The partners agree on a time span of, perhaps, one or two minutes. On the command, 'Now', A closes his eyes and senses the duration of time (without moving) until another command, 'Stop'. Repeat the procedure several times.

Now, when A is ready, he or she will no longer stand still but will improvise movements, attempting to come to an end when they think the set time is up. The timekeeper will see if A's estimate of the time duration tallies. Again, this exercise should be repeated many times.

Discrepancies in timing can be overcome not by adding to, or cutting out, movement, but rather by working on, and enhancing, the expressive qualities of the existing movements.

This exercise can be done with speech. The same rules apply. Remember, we look upon voice as an extension of movement. It may help to move and speak simultaneously. We are not aiming to add more speech and movement, or less, we are searching for expressiveness within the exercise. Perhaps some movements or words will become more sudden and others, more sustained.

Success will come with greater expression. Don't confuse this with acting yet. However, you will be aware that the seeds of characterisation have been planted and it is an important step on the way to role experimentation.

Exercise 4

Many 'timing' games can be played with a stopwatch. For example, try timing your earlier locomotion improvisations on Page 48.

Exercise 5
Individual work for any number of students. Spread out in the room and turn around with arms outstretched, making sure your own kinesphere is not overlapped.

A (i) Stance. Make a fast movement of short duration into any direction. (A fast movement will tend to be of short duration but as we saw in Exercise 2, fast and slow are relative terms when applied to individuals.) I tend to stress that a movement must be exaggeratedly fast or slow. However, the important aspect here is to experience the dynamic quality of suddenness. Repeat the sudden movement in another direction. It is essential to try all these movements out with various parts of the body leading and also with the whole body moving simultaneously.
(ii) Try this exercise with a word or a sound accompanying the movement.

B (i) Stance. Make a movement which accelerates during its short duration, sensing the increasing 'suddenness'. Repeat in different directions.
(ii) Try with accompanying sound.

C (i) Stance. Make a slow movement of longer duration, sensing the sustained quality. Repeat in different directions.
(ii) Try with accompanying sound.

D (i) Stance. Make a decelerating movement of longer duration, sensing its 'sustained' quality. Repeat in different directions.
(ii) With sound.

The sustained movements could also be accompanied by a singing tone. If anyone has difficulty with the qualities of suddenness or sustainment, a pianist could be of great help. However, the actor should bear in mind that, sooner or later, he will have to overcome this difficulty for himself. Rhythm is not about doing a little tap number in time and then discarding it with the end of the dance. It is the sensing within us of a quality that we share with all living matter. There is no need to worry. The training will help to extend your range of movement. Enjoy moving and don't intellectualise at the expense of your body training. There are other combinations such as:

E (i) Stance. Fast movement of long duration.
    (ii) Stance. Acceleration over long duration.
    We tend to think of such movements as repetitive: running, hurdling, spinning, speaking, (possibly in gibberish) with gestures.

F (i) Stance. A short slow movement.
    (ii) A short deceleration.
    These are more difficult to sense (to be aware of) and when observed, usually appear as transitions. Try them out as links between the other exercises. This should be done, initially, between two movements of the same expressive quality. Later, experiment with contrasting qualities:
    Example. A sustained movement of longer duration, as in C(i). Transition: A short deceleration. F(ii).
    Fast movement of long duration. E(i).
    Transition: A short slow movement. F(i).
    Finish with B(i) – an acceleration of short duration. This sudden quality can give a purposeful end to the movement improvisation. You can experiment, making up many other interesting combinations.

Mobility and Attention to Detail

Remember that your kinesphere surrounds you and therefore, you should attempt movements travelling in all directions. It is not enough to take the easy way, i.e. an arm movement travelling forward in a leisurely manner! Hopefully, your studies will have already led to some imaginative ideas but keep them for the end of the class. The movement jigsaw is not yet complete! The permutations will lead to an endless variety of expression and don't forget, the improvisations can be done with any number of people. I would suggest the group is kept fairly small in the beginning. When you have managed the exercises with some success, try improvising on Example C (i), F(ii), E(i) and F(i) above. For instance, the given circumstances could be:

(a) A man talking about his dog and the short transitional movements could be asides to the dog or vice versa! Other possibilities that spring to mind are, perhaps:
(b) A dinner party with a woman making conversation to a man on either side of her,

(c) Two men talking to each other over her head or trying to see each other by twisting round her; (transitional moments either by the woman or the alternate man).

Get it right technically, initially, and then end the session by 'taking it away'! It should be an enjoyable and informed experience! You may not always be exact but you will be much more aware of the qualities of suddenness and sustainment. Use your own imagination to invent further given circumstances!

Further Exploration

These exercises should enrich the actors' movement vocabulary during improvisation. 'Given circumstances' should be kept simple, movements curtailed to normal, everyday working actions and when using the voice, start with gibberish. Tools and props are helpful.

Reminder

The kinesthetic sense can be likened to the weaving tentacles of an octopus. Information is relayed to the brain about the state of the body and its ongoing relationship with the outside world. This constant awareness of the current 'state of play', enables the brain to assess the situation and take appropiate action, i.e. unity of mind and body (gestalt). The resulting behaviour is a universal movement language which can be interpreted by others and lead to a reaction on their part.

Chapter 8

Weight

Our ability to stand upright depends on the tension between the upward force of our bodies and the downward pull of gravity. When something occurs to affect this vertical, upward/downward balance, such as illness or drunkenness, we tend to 'lose balance' as a direct result of this unequal tension.

Although this upward force is unconscious for the most part, if we lose consciousness it will betray us. For instance, in the case of faintness, there is the progressive diminishing of counter-balance as the body succumbs entirely to gravitational thrust, sinking to the floor, no longer able to support its own weight. Secondly, in the case of drunkenness there is the feeling of the three-dimensional world constantly shifting. Attempts to remain upright will be thwarted as perception of the vertical, up/down dimension falters. The drunkard, too, will probably sink to the floor!

As you have seen, when starting any movement exercise, we preface the instructions: 'take stance'. Standing upright, with the weight evenly and lightly distributed on both feet, clears the mind and body for action. Leaning against a wall, supporting the weight on one foot only and thinking of lunch is not a disciplined way to work. It may well be that the physical movement you are about to do, will require you then to take up this starting position. But the activity of needing to move into a position of leaning against a wall, balancing on one leg, will be the result of kinesthetic sensing and not inertia. The mind will be fully engaged and lunch forgotten!

I have mentioned the necessity of balancing the gravitational pull against an equal upward force and the collapse of the body when this isn't there. Moving the body anywhere in space requires energy along a light to strong continuum. A small upward bounce would need only light force whereas a pole vaulter needs to use much more energy and, therefore, stronger force. Because the body senses the changes of force in these movements, we call this energy kinetic force.

Even when the body appears static, i.e. in a held position, force is required to maintain the 'hold'. (I am reminded of Howard Goorney playing a catatonic in Theatre Workshop's production of Ewan MacColl's *The Other Animals*. He was able to hold his position for long periods at a stretch.) Anyone who has ever had to keep their arms outstretched for any length of time will know the feeling of weariness as they strive to maintain enough tension to keep up the position. When tired, the body gives way to the pull of gravity.

There is also the force we use against individuals and objects. Giving a gentle push to a small child requires a much lighter force than helping to push a grand piano across a room. Both offer external resistance, but in one, it is lightly overcome. In the other, much greater energy is needed. In both cases, it is applied directly to the external resistance.

Examples of contrasting light and strong exertions are as follows:

Weight and the Pull of Gravity

1. (a) Exceptionally lightly held stance (lightly anti-gravity), the weight a little forward on the toes.

(b) Exaggerated pulling upward, (strongly anti-gravity), of the body away from the force of gravity. The skeletal frame, like a piece of elastic, is pulled further apart than in (a).

Weight and Kinetic Force in Movements of the Body

2. (a) Light movements in any direction. This lightness is relative, depending on the size of the body part moving and its manoeuvrability but there will be just enough exertion to keep the sensation of lightness throughout the movement. This is light kinetic force.

(b) Strong movements of the body and its parts are the result of kinetic sensing. When the movement is slow and strong, the force is felt as an inner, centralised strength. When a large movement is quick and strong, the feeling is one of strength, and is often the result of an urgent need to change an existing condition.

Weight and Static Force

3. (a) Light static force of sufficient degree to counter-balance or provide a light tension.

(b) Strong static tension is often used in 'held' positions. It can also accompany strong kinetic force. (See 2(b).)

Weight and External Resistance
4(a) Light minimal force against outside resistance.
   (b) Strong maximum force against outside resistance.

Exercise 1
(i) Ref. (1a). Take stance. Now lighten the upward force, your heels barely touching the floor. The impression an observer will have is of light preparedness, of readiness for immediate action as in dance or boxing. Lightness occurs when the upward exertion and the downward pull of gravity are evenly matched.
(ii) Ref. (1b). Exaggerate the above exercise, stretching the body further upward, away from the gravitational pull. The resulting position will be ludicrous, creating a comical impression. Without a kinetic bounce, a parachute or the benefit of 'Kirby's flying wires', we will never overcome the force of gravity.

Exercise 2
(i) Ref. (2a). Stance. Imagine you are on a short ladder. A partner will hand up imaginary Christmas tree decorations from different locations around the ladder. Some of the decorations will be light, small and very fragile. Others will be relatively less light and a little larger. Don't forget the fairy who goes on the top of the tree. Select the right amount of energy, i.e. kinetic force, to turn, twist, balance, reach out, take hold of, carry and position the object on the tree. All movements will be light. But there will be degrees of lightness – remember our continuum. The handing over of the different objects will be at different levels, different distances from the ladder and positioned around the back half of your kinesphere.
(ii) Ref. (2b). Imagine you are travelling by bus in the rush hour. You are forced to stand. The driver keeps stopping and starting, throwing you off-balance and you are trying to find support somewhere. A light or strong anti-gravity exertion as in Exercise 1(i) and (ii) would be useless. Even a light static exertion as in Exercise 2(i) would not help. A strong kinetic force would be better. Sense the direction and position to take up and when to adjust your balance. All this can occur in a

very small area. When the motion of the bus is sustained, your strong kinetic stance may appear as almost static. But a sudden jolt may give rise to a sharp, involuntary, large movement, leaving you partially off-balance. Perhaps you were momentarily inattentive or unable to keep up a strong stance. It is likely then that your 'movement' jolt will be strong, because of the lack of counter-tension, the bus's own motion meeting little resistance on your part.

Exercise 3

(i) Imagine you are waiting for someone or something to appear. You may be ready to greet them or you may be prepared to take flight, if necessary. Light static force will be experienced as you wait expectantly using minimal tension or counter-tension.

(ii) Strong static tension can be accompanied by strong kinetic force as we have seen in Exercise 2(ii). Another experience of static tension for you to try would be the 'held' position a weight-lifter achieves before or after the wobbling has stopped. Children play a game of 'Statues'. When the music stops, they take up the most bizarre positions and hold them, with grim determination, producing strong counter-tension. If they wobble they're out. Try it!

Exercise 4

(i) Light minimal force against outside resistance is to be seen in a game of 'Tiggy' where you have to touch someone who then has to charge after someone else and try to 'tig' them. Tiddley Winks is another good example. The fun for the actor in all these examples is that excitement often swells and tempers fray, resulting in less than 'light minimal force' being used! A more sober example would be to follow Voltaire's *Candide*, in gently tending his seedlings.

(ii) Strong energetic interaction against outside resistance can be seen in driving off in golf, kicking a football, pushing a car or losing your temper in Tiddley Winks and giving your opponent a clout!

Chapter 9

*A Survey of the Space, Time, Weight,
and Flow Continuums*

In my early days with Laban, I worked with engineers and factory consultants. After introducing them to Laban's work through a course of intensive movement training, we formed a team and visited factories eager to try out our advanced ideas to improve productivity.

My own job was to observe, analyse and notate the movement performance of the workers in the various departments or workshops. It meant learning the different tasks as quickly and efficiently as I could and selecting the most appropriate efforts for each action. Some workers could not keep up their initial speedy activity and faded rapidly after a couple of hours. It was nearing the end of the war and output was still of the utmost importance.

At one factory, I found a young woman who seemed to approach her job in almost too leisurely or 'laid-back' fashion. Nevertheless, it was precisely this performance, maintained at a steady pace throughout each day, that always yielded the highest output. She also seemed far less exhausted than her colleagues. It did not take me long, through our movement classes, to encourage the others to adapt their efforts, especially when the results were seen to be so successful. Another part of my class was devoted to compensatory exercise; often dance themes using the whole body. In this case, I concentrated on strong, free rhythms to offset sitting at a conveyor belt all day. Occasionally it was necessary to advise switching personnel from one workshop to another, when those preferring a freer, irregular rhythm would leave the predictable rhythm of the conveyor belt, which governed the timing of their actions, and move into an operational sphere where the individual freedom to move around at will was far more congenial to them. My fifty-minute classes were taken during normal working hours. Even so, there was no drop in performance levels. On the contrary, after three weeks, the output increased dramatically.

Of course, not all my work was in industry. Like all pioneers, I was sent to follow up a great variety of calls asking for more information about Laban's work. I seemed to cover most of England during these years. One of the jobs that brought me the greatest pleasure was my stay at Dartington Hall in Devon. I arranged a variety of classes for office workers, landgirls, the Forestry Corps, the singers, dancers and musicians of the Arts department and textile workers. In whatever spare time I had, I was busy improvising dances to the accompaniment of young musicians.

Although I was never to return to industry after joining Theatre Workshop, this early and unique opportunity to observe and analyse the actions of many people in a variety of very different occupations, served me well when I came to work with actors and dancers in the theatre. It meant that I was quickly able to recognise problems and help with characterisation amongst other things.

I have already briefly mentioned the use of movement notation in my work. At that time, our industrial notation symbols differed from the dance symbols. Thanks to Albrecht Knust, one of Laban's earliest pupils in Germany, we now have a comprehensive and authoritative notation for all movement. Valuable contributions have also been made by Anne Hutcheson in the US and Valerie Preston-Dunlop in the UK. An example of notation was given to you on page 30, when I introduced the Dimensional Scale.

Of course, it is not necessary for actors (or indeed many dancers), to have an intensive knowledge of notation; for choreographers I believe it to be essential. However, many of my students have found it invaluable to be able to use a basic shorthand in the margin of a script as a guideline towards interpreting a character's movement behaviour. More dancers are also coming to realise that it is not enough to generalise over a role; like actors, they need to work hard at discovering the feelings and motivation of the character they are portraying in dance. More about this later.

Now we have studied the continuums separately through the past four chapters, let us take two of them simultaneously and see what mysteries unfold and how easy it is to write a simple shorthand notation for personal use. The journey continues!

We know that the four motion factors, Space, Time, Weight and Flow can influence the movement and attitude of an individual. Any action requires, however, not the use of one continuum, but of all four. It is not possible to read a book, take a bath, play a game or listen to music without using Time. We use the Space within our kinesphere, (even in sitting or standing still) and we counterbalance our movements, using the right amount of energy (Weight) for specific actions. The important point to remember here, is that not all continuums are necessarily stressed. One can stress just one factor such as Time, or two factors, Weight-Space or three factors as in Space-Time-Weight. Laban called the following symbol 'a simple device'. It links two movement factors, Weight and Flow, but does not show us their exact degree along the continuum.

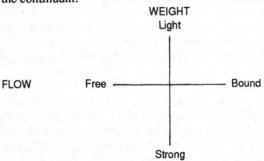

The above diagram gives rise to four movement permutations:

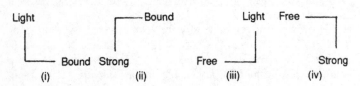

Example 1
Swinging a heavy object with (i) light-bound, (ii) strong-bound or (iii) light-free effort would be inappropriate. We would need to use a strong-free effort as in (iv).

This was brought home to me quite forcibly when I was working with the girls of the Forestry Corps at Dartington. I had to show them how to wield heavy, long-handled axes. Whilst swinging the axe in a sideways direction, we swung our bodies in a forward/backward direction to give more weight to the moment of impact when we met outside resistance, i.e. scrub that had been allowed to grow too high. As we moved in a long line, spread out through the woods, we started to sing, the rhythm keeping us all together. It also helped us to concentrate; the axes were extremely heavy and very sharp!

This strong-free effort would, of course, be a disaster to someone placing fragile decorations on a Christmas tree from the top of a ladder. In this case, the most appropriate combination would be the light-bound (i) effort.

But what of the space continuum? Well, we know that a swinging object will describe a definite curve in space. So that when we came to axe the trees at Dartington, we made no attempt to minimise the curve or to exaggerate it. We sensed the direction and moved the top part of our bodies with it while the legs moved in an harmonious counter-tension.

Example 2

We have learnt that the body also moves in natural arcs. Placing a fragile decoration like the Christmas fairy, which has to go exactly on top of the tree, we need to be fairly direct. A particular spot on a small branch is our goal. There is no need to 'smell the flowers'! That would be a waste of time and energy. We could also knock other decorations over if we were too indirect. Even so, we know that, in order to be fairly direct, our arm will still be using three dimensions simultaneously although only one direction is stressed Space is indicated thus, on our effort-graph:

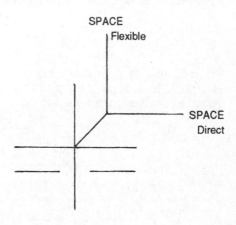

SPACE
Flexible

SPACE
Direct

71

The small diagonal linking the three continuums, Space, Weight and Time is used as the sign of effort. On the preceding page, Example 1, I suggested that the best effort to use in swinging a heavy weight would be:

i.e. Free in Flow and Strong in Weight. But what of the spatial quality? Well, we know it will naturally describe a curved path and too direct a movement would be inappropriate – in the case of my Forestry Corps girls, positively dangerous! So the effort-graph:

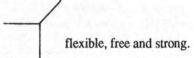

would be quite inappropriate, because of its spatial directness.

The most appropriate effort would be:

flexible, free and strong.

Returning to the Christmas tree and its decorations. We decided that lightness and boundness were appropriate, recorded as:

We know that the movement needs to be fairly direct; anything else would be a waste of energy and inefficient. Therefore, the proper recorded effort-graph would be:

and not

Finally, we must consider the Time continuum and its role within the effort-graph. It is included thus:

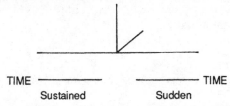

TIME ———————   ——————— TIME
      Sustained   Sudden

Once again, I will remind you of the heavy swinging object. The movement could not be executed satisfactorily with too sustained a tempo. In the case of the Forestry Corps, the axes were heavy for women and we had to adapt to the increasing tempo of the curving fall of the blade as it descended. I remember my first attempt at using an axe. On all previous occasions, I had used a croquet mallet for practice, becoming so adept at the exercise that when presented with the axe, I was not at all fazed. An over-confident teenager, I swung the axe with complete sangfroid – a perfect working action which only missed my left foot by a hair's breadth! My flow was exaggeratedly free and employment of weight too light! I had not taken into account the need to adjust my efforts to the different tool. So the following recorded effort would be wrong and dangerous:

The most appropriate effort would be:

(a)

Finally, too speedy a placing of the fairy on the Christmas tree could demolish much of your earlier work, scattering decorations in all directions. Care is needed and this involves taking a little more time. Hence, we should not choose to use the effort-graph:

73

but

(b)

which is far more appropriate.

Our complete effort-graph, containing all four continuums, now looks like this:

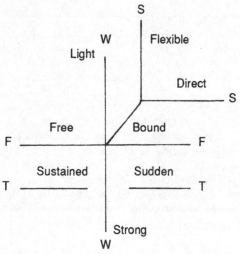

However, I mentioned earlier that it is not always necessary to consider all four motion factors. Indeed, basic working actions can be expressed through the use of only three exertions, Weight, Space and Time.

Let us look at our two examples again, this time omitting the Flow factor:

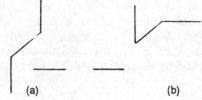

(a)   (b)

It is obvious they have nothing in common. Their elements are completely contrasting.

(a) Swinging a heavy object demands
    strong, flexible, sudden exertion
(b) Depositing a light object carefully demands
    light, direct, sustained exertion.

Trying to find one word to encapsulate each of the exertions (a) and (b) is very difficult. There are far more movements than there are words to describe them. The best way I can explain it is to imagine that we are looking at the elements from the polar opposites of each continuum. So (a) would be seen as very strong, very flexible, very sudden and (b) as very light, very direct, very sustained. In this way the (a) exertion becomes a slashing effort whilst (b) becomes a gliding effort. What we must bear in mind is that more appropriate words for slashing and gliding might be found if one varied the degrees of any one, or all, of their continuums. I will come to this later. But in starting out, I find it is best to go for the polar extremes in each case. After all, we are in the introductory stage and these are the BASIC efforts on which our movement studies rest. This leads us finally to an introduction of the eight basic combinations of Weight, Space and Time.

The Eight Basic Efforts

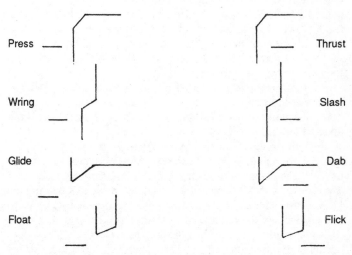

Press

Wring

Glide

Float

Thrust

Slash

Dab

Flick

It is possible for a working action to require two or more efforts for it to be successfully accomplished. If the swinging object were a heavy parcel that had to be placed on a high shelf, the slashing effort could be followed with a pressing effort which would push or slide the parcel onto the waiting shelf. A very strong, muscular person might just prefer to press-lift the weight straightaway. Alternatively, the light object could be a tiny ball of cotton wool, representing snow, which could be lightly thrown with a flicking movement onto a branch of the tree instead of the previous gliding effort used for the fairy.

In these examples we see the beginnings of preference which has to do with personality.

Some people may prefer to use a slashing effort and others a pressing effort, in the first example. In the second, a person might prefer to use a sustained and direct gliding effort, rather than a quick and flexible flicking movement. In each case, the movements are appropriate to the task and, therefore, people are free to choose the effort most appropriate to their own personality. It would be wrong and inappropriate if an habitual 'glider' were to choose a flicking effort to accomplish the task on a regular basis. Where strength is required to fulfil working actions, one would not select those who preferred lightness of touch as the norm . . . any more than one would normally expect a navvy to be skilled at embroidery. (I am awaiting a reader's first letter, telling me of their talented uncle who is just such a phenomenon!) Where a job offers no scope for an individual to use his own abilities and no time for training can be given, it is better to find a different job for the employee. This is what I did in our first factory with one or two of the older women who found the work load too heavy for them.

But performers are a different breed! No easy option for them! It is essential that they extend their personal ability range and become equally skilled in all the basic efforts. At least, that is the aim and we can go a long way to achieving it.

Remember then, efforts can be appropriate or inappropriate either to the job in hand or to the person performing the task, or to both. The choice depends upon a conscious selection of effort. These efforts can be performed with or without stressing the Flow factor which can also add to the appropriateness or inappropriateness of the effort used to accomplish the task.

A job requiring one to twist material into a precise shape would need a bound wringing effort whereas slinging ropes together across a void would probably need more fluency, a freer approach.

The shorthand notation taken from the effort-graph in the above examples would look like this:

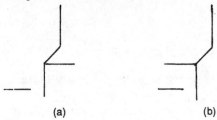

(a) Twisting material into precise shape, and (b) slinging ropes across a void.

For the performer, it is essential to learn to control the Flow factor. By that, I mean that you must be able to use free flow and bound flow as appropriate, at will.

Chapter 10

Exploratory Exercises for Each of the
Eight Basic Effort Actions

Pressing: Direct, Sustained, Strong
This movement is one of obvious bound flow.
1. Feel it first with the palms of the hands. Then take the movement into a simultaneous forward, downward zone, diagonally across the body. Now extend your pressing activity into all spatial directions and into high, medium and low zones.
2. Let other parts of the body lead in pressing, for example, the back, the knees, the top of the head, the elbows or the feet.
3. Let two parts of the body press simultaneously in two different directions, for example, the right palm upwards and the left hip downwards.
4. Press simultaneously in three different directions, for example, head backward, hips forwards and elbows outwards, away from their own sides.
5. Press down with the feet as they walk, taking the body in different directions.
6. Try pressing in kneeling, sitting and lying positions as well as standing.
7. Try pressing as a transition from one position to another.
8. Try exercises 5, 6 and 7 combined with 3 and 4.

Note. The permutations are endless. Try all the exercises as often as you can before attempting to use the pressing effort in an improvisation. I want you to feel the basic quality of the movement without any considerations of circumstances or of characterisation. However, it would be useful to accompany the movement with voice at a later stage in the exercises. These recommendations go for all the eight basic efforts. When it is time to improvise your dance or dramatic situation, remember you will naturally move in and out of the pressing action. You must consciously select moments in which the action is specifically pressing and keep to them in any one exercise. Be ingenious in your use of the kinesphere.

In an everyday situation, an acting improvisation or even in dance, one can push against a concrete object and feel its resistance. (Remember the piano?) In a more imaginary situation, with no concrete object in view, the performer will use 'antagonistic muscle' groups to provide resistance. A counter-tension is set up in other parts of the body, giving a feeling of controlled strength. This feeling parallels the feeling of controlled strength experienced when moving the piano, or any other concrete object, even gently pushing a child. In the latter case it would, of course, be much diminished.

When engaged in very strong resistance in one clear direction as in the piano example, we are said to be 'fighting against' Weight and Space. At the same time we are 'indulging in' Time, sustaining the action over a period of time.

The effort of strong muscular tension results in strong, firm movements. Other such examples, apart from pulling, are thrusting, slashing and wringing.

Flicking: Flexible, Sudden, Light
This is a movement with obvious free flow.
1. Imagine a fly alighting on food or dust on your jacket. Flick it away with your hands by quickly twisting the wrists and fingers.
2. Move on to flicking in every part of your kinesphere, near to the body, far away, use high, medium and low zones, directions should include backward (behind) and forward (in front) and sideways.
3. Try flicking with your shoulders, head and feet. The most important zone for flicking hands is high, outwards and backwards. But it is essential to try it in all directions, with the hands working simultaneously or alternatively, in the same, or in different, directions.
4. Continue the exploration with flicking by involving the elbows, hips and knees.
5. Try jumping, flicking the feet in the air. Flicking the feet rhythmically on the floor gives rise to a light tap dance effect or a 'soft shoe shuffle'.
6. As in pressing, flicking can be performed in kneeling, sitting or lying positions and be used as a transition from one position to another.

7. Repeated flicking produces a fluttering movement. When the whole body is involved, there is a sense of intense lightness and buoyancy. Laban had a party trick of fluttering his hand so quickly that a finger and thumb seemed to disappear.

Whereas in pressing, we need to do battle against outside resistance by 'fighting' against Weight, in flicking we can yield to the feeling of lightness, thereby 'indulging in' Weight i.e. decreasing resistance.

Similarly, the flicking action, in its flexible use of Space, yields to a many-directional approach ('smelling the flowers'), and encourages 'indulgence' in Space; very different from the one-directional experience of pressing.

However, any indulgence in Time, as in pressing, is now firmly resisted. The flicking action is very brief – 'gone in a flash'. Therefore, we say that we are fighting against Time in this action.

Flicking is not an action of relaxed shaking. Crispness accompanies lightness, producing just enough counter-tension to enhance these qualities.

Muscular relaxation prevails because of the lightness of the movement, whereas in pressing, we were very conscious of muscular tension. It should be understood that muscular relaxation does not lead to 'floppy' action but that the degree of counter-tension, whilst being extremely light, is just enough to maintain the crisp quality of flicking.

Lightness is sometimes referred to as 'fine touch'. Other 'fine touch' actions include light stirring, floating, gliding, dabbing, wafting and tapping. Do not be put off by the fact that I have added a few derivatives to the eight basic actions. I will clarify them later.

Wringing: Flexible, Sustained, Strong
Wringing is usually performed with bound flow.
1. Try the movement in the hands first, as if wringing out clothes.
2. Imagine you are, literally, a wet blanket and try wringing yourself out! For exercise purposes, practise wringing in a deep, forward and outward zone. Of course, you must attempt the movement with both the right and then the left side leading.
3. Try wringing in all zones and all directions of the kinesphere.
4. Remember to try simultaneous and alternate movements of different parts of the body into different directions or into the same direction.

5. Stand, lie, sit or kneel to perform the action and use it as a transitional movement from one position to another.

There are many examples of wringing where concrete resistance by an object is offered, such as washing, knotting, twisting or untangling ropes. Where no such concrete resistance exists, strong counter-tension is necessary and can be felt throughout the body.

In wringing, one is 'fighting against' resistance in Weight but 'indulging in' Space and Time and yielding to flexibility and sustainment of the movement.

Flexibility of movement relies on sets of muscles able to bring about continuous changes in direction. Other examples of flexible actions are slashing, floating and flicking.

Dabbing: Direct, Sudden, Light

The basic effort of dabbing is usually performed with free flow but can, when necessary, also be performed with bound flow. I would suggest from the outset that you first explore all the possibilities of each exercise with free flow and then repeat them using bound flow.

1. This action is clearly felt in the hands as in a painter dabbing at a canvas or in typing. Try dabbing with the right side leading across the body, diagonally backwards, over the opposite shoulder. Repeat with the left side leading.
2. Dab with the feet. It is easy to quickly point the heels or toes. Again, try in all directions and all zones.
3. Try with the knees, hips, shoulders, head, elbows, chin, back and chest. Take plenty of time to experience dabbing in all these parts of the body. Some parts will lend themselves more easily to the effort than others but that is no excuse for not working away at the more difficult movements. It could be that you are particularly stiff in these areas. Remember that you are intent also on extending your own range of movement as a performer.

Do not forget to try simultaneous and alternate movements.
4. Try the action with steps. Knees can dab upwards and toes or heels downwards.
5. When dabbing at a concrete object, (canvas, typewriter), we experience resistance. However, dabbing in the air requires our muscles to produce the necessary counter-tension which

81

can be felt throughout the body even if only one finger is involved in the action.

In this action we are 'indulging in' Weight, yielding to a feeling of lightness. On the other hand, we are 'fighting against' resisting Space and Time.

A unilateral muscular function always prevails in direct movement. Gliding, thrusting, punching and pressing are some other examples of direct movement. Extreme directness does not allow for plasticity.

Slashing: Sudden, Strong, Flexible

Slashing is usually performed with free flow which tends to fade out into floating.

1. A good pathway in which to experience the feeling of slashing is from high forward, across the body to downwards, outwards and backwards. One arm should lead the effort. Then change to the other.
2. Try the arms slashing separately in all directions.
3. Now try each leg separately.
4. Continue with all the possibilities mentioned for the other actions, i.e. limbs separately or together, kneeling sitting, lying or standing; all directions, including inwards and outwards and moving in different zones.
5. Use slashing as a transition from one position to another.
6. Large jumps give good opportunities for slashing movements of the legs, arms or trunk.

Slashing aimed at a concrete object encounters resistance. The great freedom of this action in the air requires various muscle groups to provide a strong counter-tension.

The action of slashing is one of 'fighting against' Weight and Time but 'indulging' in Space. Again multi-lateral counter-tensions prevail when we 'indulge' in Space. If we do so with strength, we enter a flexible fluency, or free flow. It would be hard to stop the effort at any given moment. When the strength fades and Time slows towards the end of the action, the movement becomes floating.

Other fluent actions are flicking and thrusting. When the action of thrusting fades, losing strength and slowing down, it becomes gliding.

It is important to remember that slashing is usually performed with free flow. However, when it fades into floating, the flow can then become bound or remain free.

Gliding: Sustained, Light, Direct

Gliding is usually performed with bound flow.

1. Imagine you are smoothing something horizontally, the palms of the hands parallel with the floor or vertically, with the palms facing forward. Or again, let the palms face inwards as one removes imaginary cobwebs in front of the body. The most important zone is across the body diagonally forward high but, as with the other efforts, you must take the exercise into all zones, all directions, using different parts of the body, some simultaneously, some alternately.
2. Alternate legs can glide over the floor as steps or gestures through space.
3. Gliding with the trunk results in a smooth swaying movement.
4. Remember it can also be used as a transition from one position to another.

   In gliding along a concrete object we meet with resistance. Gliding in the air brings about a counter-tension felt throughout the whole body, giving the feeling of controlled boundness. As a result, the movement can be stopped at any given moment. Bound movements in the air rely on the antagonistic muscles to control the action.

   Other actions tending to be bound are those of wringing and pressing and their derivatives. Thrusting can be performed with bound or free flow.

   The action of gliding 'fights against' Space but 'indulges in' Weight and Time.

Thrusting or Punching: Direct, Sudden, Strong

Thrusting can be performed with bound or free flow.

1. Try making a fist of the hands and punch forcibly at some imaginary object. The main zone for this exercise is punching with one arm and fist across the body attacking a target deep (low) backward.
2. Thrusting(punching) with the legs becomes stamping.
3. Try with other parts of the body, head-butting, elbows, shoulders, knees and hips.
4. Explore your kinesphere in all directions and zones, using the parts of your body simultaneously or alternately. One doesn't need to remain standing. It is possible to punch in a kneeling, lying or sitting position. In a lying position, the feet can punch into the air.

With a real target, one encounters a natural resistance; the most obvious examples are a punch-bag used by boxers or two fighters in the ring. Where there is no concrete object to resist our punch, we need the counter-tension of the antagonistic muscles which should be felt throughout the body, no matter what part of it is leading the action.

The essential characteristics in punching involve 'fighting against' Weight, Space and Time. Therefore, there is no 'indulgence' in this action, no yielding either to lightness or flexibility and no yielding to sustainment of the movement.

An abrupt or sudden muscular reaction prevails in quick movements, including such actions as flicking, slashing, dabbing and, of course, thrusting.

Floating: Flexible, Sustained, Light

Floating can be performed with bound or free flow.

1. The action of floating is felt momentarily in a leap when the energy for take-off has subsided and before descent occurs. On waking, one can also experience it as a slight 'stirring' of the resting body during respiration.
2. The most important zone for floating is high, forwards and outwards.
3. Now try floating in all directions and zones as in previous effort exercises.
4. Try floating downwards as well as upwards, with different parts of the body leading alternately or simultaneously.
5. Float or fly with the legs or touch the floor very lightly on tip-toe.
6. Attempt the effort sitting, lying and kneeling as well as standing.
7. Use floating as a transition from one of these positions to another.

If one needs to use floating as in very lightly stirring a liquid, then the liquid is an object offering resistance, however slight. Without any external resistance, as in a leap through the air, the body employs sets of muscles in a counter-tension, thereby helping to overcome the weight of the body momentarily. The tensions must be kept to a minimum to achieve a floating movement.

In this action there is no 'fighting against'. Here all is 'indulgence', i.e. the essence of floating is one of 'indulging in' or yielding to Time, Weight and Space. We indulge in our lightness, sustain our movement and wander around 'smelling our flowers' in Space.

Counter-tensions are very slight and multi-lateral in floating but nonetheless sustain the muscular function of the effort. Pressing, gliding, wringing and their derivatives are all examples of sustained actions.

Chapter 11

Intermission

*followed by an introduction to the inter-relationship
of the Eight Basic Effort Actions.*

Sometimes on a long journey, it is necessary to pause for a while
and look more closely at the map. Let us now do that. Initially,
your aim may have been to travel from town 'A' to a village 'B'.
You have already checked the grid and the direction on the map
and it is, say, south, south west. North always remains constant
on your compass bearing, therefore, all the other directions
including south south west will remain constant. You will expect
this to be so; after all, this is the general space outside your
kinesphere. It does not alter because you have turned your head
or body to face another direction.

Town and village may grow and shrink according to a shifting
population but the distance from centre to centre will remain
constant at 'X' number of miles. Taking the main route, i.e. the
motorway, is probably the most direct way to proceed if you are
like many travellers and only concerned in completing your
journey quickly. Travelling at a given speed over 'X' number of
miles enables you to deduce how long the journey will take. In
this case, the time factor is also constant.

But look again at your ordnance survey map. What do these
little signs mean and what sort of country do the secondary roads
pass through? What is this bridle path through the forest like and
how high is that mountain? Wouldn't it be a pity to miss this
panoramic view denoted by a 'sunburst' sign? (Just as you have
your movement notation, so cartographers have their signs.)
What caused the earth to erupt, throwing up that mass of rock set
at an extraordinary angle? Why don't you take longer over the
journey and learn more about the nature of this countryside;
experience the harmony of a natural world untouched by the
mechanical   digger.   You   might   just   make   exciting   new

discoveries for yourself which would lead to greater physical, mental and spiritual fulfilment. This route may take a little longer to explore but the 'beaten track' of the motorway is 'beaten' from the start and leaves nothing to the imagination.

What has all this to do with the dimensional cross and the cube? Well, we are all travellers making our own way through life. Some of us have eyes only for the goal ahead and take no interest in other travellers or in the surrounding landscape. As a result, we learn very little on the way and arrive unaware and impoverished from so many missed opportunities.

It is the wealth of detail in the ordnance survey map that is of such great value and pleasure to the dedicated walker. And so it is with the art of movement traveller who leaves the dour town of Stir-halt and heads for the beautiful city of Spatial Harmony. Aware of his kinship with the natural laws in nature, he is eager to explore all the exciting spatial pathways criss-crossing his kinesphere, knowing that they will lead to a greater understanding of the mastery of movement. With this in mind, let us have a brief look over our shoulder before continuing the journey.

The six fundamental directions of the Dimensional Scale also contain their own dynamic qualities, giving rise to such feelings as:
1. Lightness, associated with upward or High direction.
2. Strength, associated with downward or Deep direction.
3. Restriction. A movement across the body, producing a. straight or Direct movement.
4. Freedom of movement associated with the body's open side, leading to Flexibility.
5. Suddenness as in fear, resulting in the body's contraction Backward.
6. Sustainment, as tension is slowly released, leading the body in the opposite direction, i.e. Forwards.

Laban called these dynamic qualities 'secondary tendencies'.

Whilst you can, of course, attempt any dynamic action in any direction; for example, Lightness in a downward movement or Suddenness in a forward movement. it is better to start by becoming proficient in the natural order as practised in the Dimensional scale.

The labile quality of the Diagonal scale produces feelings of great excitement as the body moves along pure diagonal pathways, simultaneously influenced by all three dimensions. (RHF/LDB, LHB/RDF, LHF/RDB and RHB/LDF.)

A study of the Space, Time, Weight and Flow continuums led to the introduction of eight basic effort actions and the Effort-graph.

Just as there were 'sunbursts' in the imaginary journey I described earlier, I would now like to introduce you to a 'sunburst' in your art of movement studies. The diagram of the cube below is, of course, familiar; as is the dimensional cross. I hope by putting one inside the other, it will give you a clearer view of what we call the 'dynamosphere'. You will see that the cube of the dynamosphere can be correlated to the cube of the kinesphere.

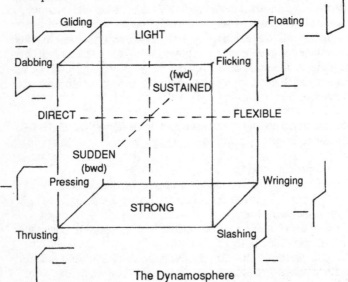

The Dynamosphere

The ceiling and the floor of the cube represent the two polar extremes of the Weight continuum, i.e. light and strong.

The forward and backward panels represent the two polar extremes of the Time continuum, i.e. sustained and sudden.

The two side panels represent the two polar extremes of the Space continuum, i.e. direct and flexible. Leading with the left side of the body would mean a reversal of the direct and flexible panels and the effort actions linked with them. This is consistent with our studies of the Dimensional Scale.

You will remember that I have suggested optimum areas for practising the efforts. The above diagram should clear up any queries. Remember that we are considering the human skeleton and its three-dimensional movement 'potential'. Whilst recognising that these spatial areas seem ideally placed for the individual efforts, we must try the efforts out in all parts of the kinesphere.

Look at the top, forward, right-hand corner of the cube. From the diagram we know that, if the body is leading with the right side, the movement is flexible in Space i.e. the right side of body going to its right, its open, flexible side. It is also situated on the forward panel which makes the action sustained in Time. Finally, it is situated on the 'ceiling', which relates to Weight and is, in this case, light. The confluence of the three elements in this corner gives rise to a floating effort. Whilst you can attempt a floating effort anywhere in your dynamosphere, this area in your personal space is particularly suited to the effort. Try it out several times for yourself. (Don't forget to practise leading with your left side as well.)

A simple transition can be made from, say, i) floating to gliding or ii) pressing to wringing. In each case, only one element changes. In both examples, it is Space, as we go from flexibility to directness in the first example and from directness to flexibility in the second.

We could change the Weight element by going from dabbing to thrusting or slashing to flicking.

The Time element could be changed when going from thrusting to pressing or dabbing to gliding.

I have mentioned only a few examples. It is now your job to find the rest for yourselves. Take plenty of time to explore and be aware of the element you are changing. Work in twos and observe your partner's movements. Once again there should not be too much verbal discussion. Demonstrate in movement any point you are trying to make.

Keep the movements going to the corners of the cube during your initial experiments. It helps to establish a clear concept of the relationship of these eight basic efforts.

Try pathways taking in all eight actions, changing only one element at a time. On the whole these journeys will be fairly easy to perform in sequence, each effort having a close kinship with its predecessor.

When you have exhausted all the possibilities of one-element transitions, try changing two elements (secondary transitions.)

This means bypassing one element. For example, go from wringing to thrusting. To move as simply as possible (and not go 'round the houses'), it is necessary to go via pressing or slashing. It has been my experience that most people have their own innate preferences and choose a pathway congenial to their own effort make-up. For the performer, there is no such easy way out. The exercise must be attempted going through both transitions.

Continue to select all possible secondary transitions, always making the return journey in the opposite direction. For example: flick to glide and glide to flick. Once again, practise your observation, correcting your partner by demonstrating your point in movement.

When all such permutations have been attempted, try going through all the secondary transitions contained in the cube in sequence. One example would be: float – dab – press – slash // glide – thrust – wring – flick. You will notice that it is not possible to go right through the cube in this instance. There is a break after slash. Floating, dabbing and pressing have all been worked through. To keep to the secondary transitions, we now need to start afresh at gliding, in order to finish the circuit.

Try your own journey starting the action from a different corner. You will find the efforts will split into two parts as in the first example. With practice, one can make fairly smooth secondary transitions.

It is more difficult to make a transition when changing all the elements, i.e. going to polar opposites:

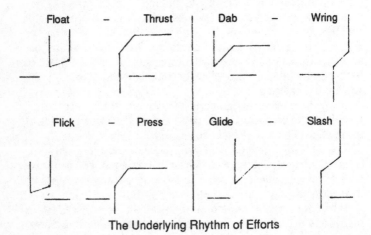

The Underlying Rhythm of Efforts

The daily actions punctuating our working life, often accompanied by expressive gestures and paralleled in the performing arts, produce rhythmic effort.

A simple working operation will probably entail preparation, one or more efforts and an end.

Pressing – Gliding

Take an everyday task like ironing. If the iron is cool, it might be necessary to use a pressing action on the object to be ironed, especially if it is damp or of thick material. When the iron reaches the correct temperature for the object, it will be much easier to iron and gliding will be the main effort. The switch from pressing to gliding is an easy transition. It changes only one element, going from 'fighting against' to 'indulging in' Weight. We could write it in notation as:

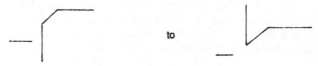

With a cooling iron, the efforts would in all probability be reversed:

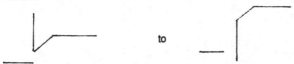

The change in Weight is most clearly felt when the efforts are performed by:
i) the same part of the body; in this case, the hand and arm lead the movement. However, it is quite possible to attempt this example, (or any other), with
ii) one part of the body employing one effort and another part of the body employing the second effort.
i) Example. A pressing ironing led by the right hand and arm, accentuated by trunk participation, followed by a gliding ironing, involving the right hand and arm only.
ii) A gliding ironing followed by a pressing step or a gliding ironing with the right hand followed by a pressing ironing with the left hand. The permutations are endless.

So far, the degree of pressing or gliding has not been mentioned.

I have been concerned with the polar extremes in all the eight basic efforts. We know that both the above examples 'indulge in' Time. They are certainly not sudden actions. On the contrary, we consider them sustained. Even so, it is possible to press or glide and be relatively long or relatively short in duration. The meaning is quite clear when you relate the rhythm of the effort to a metrical beat; one of the two combined actions might be of a shorter duration than the other even though both are sustained.

Pressing could be relatively longer than gliding which would then seem to be relatively short in comparison.

The reverse would also be true. Gliding could be seen to be relatively longer than pressing, making pressing relatively shorter in comparison.

When there is a change in Weight, as in these two combined efforts, the mover clearly experiences a decrease in strength (press – glide) or an increase (glide – press). It is a good idea to improvise simple working movements which involve these two efforts and their relative durations with awareness of their increase or decrease in strength.

Other action combinations of the same rhythm effort are:

Glide – Float   Float – Wring   Wring – Press

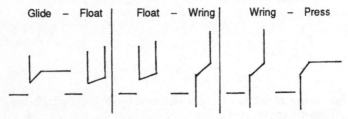

The dancer can, for instance, start like the actor with a 'working action' such as putting a milk bottle out, washing up or dusting. Working actions tend to take place mostly in front of our bodies. It is the obvious place. We face the teacher, the typewriter, the meal, the work bench, the driving wheel, the screen and so on. It is normal practice to turn to face someone talking to us. When we are not confronting objects or people and can move into the realms of fantasy, imaginatively transferring the working action anywhere else in our kinesphere, the result is dance-movement which now owes very little to its working action origin. Needless to say, the dancer, like the actor, must work through the above exercises to improve his performance and extend his range of movement.

Floating – Flicking

The combination of these two sequential actions show a difference in Time; one is sustained and one is sudden. Increase and decrease in speed will be experienced. If floating is to become of relatively very short duration, it will be observed as a mere pause or hiatus during the sequence. This is also true of all sustained efforts, i.e. pressing, gliding and wringing, as well as floating.

The flick will not lose its crisp quality unless we move so far along the Time continuum that it becomes another floating action. Other combinations of the same effort rhythm are:

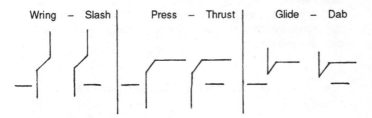

Wring – Slash   Press – Thrust   Glide – Dab

Thrusting – Slashing

The combination of these two actions in a sequence shows a difference in Space. One is direct and one is flexible. The change from directness to flexibility in the sequence and its reverse order, is powerfully felt.

The metrical rhythm will show no difference of duration in the two efforts because both are sudden. Sudden actions cannot be fundamentally increased or decreased in duration.

Other combinations of the same effort rhythm are:

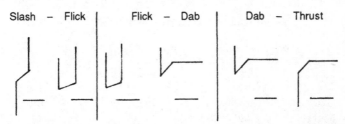

Slash – Flick   Flick – Dab   Dab – Thrust

The keen traveller on this movement journey should work through all the above rhythmic combinations, using the previous chapter where the efforts are outlined separately. Study all the possibilities and their many variations. With practice, one can

93

add to the two efforts, combining three or more in rhythmical sequence. Changes of two or three basic elements will take the mover through a choice of transitions.

Examples
a) Take pressing – floating. The most likely transitions are through gliding or wringing. (See the diagram.)
b) Or thrusting – flicking. The transitions here will most likely be dabbing or slashing. Remember, when basic efforts differ in more than one element, the transitional efforts will be more noticeable.
c) Dabbing – wringing is an example of all three elements changing. The transitions in this case could be as illustrated on the opposite page.

Gradual Changes Involving One Element

	Time	*Weight*	*Space*
Float	Flick	Wring	Glide
Thrust	Press	Dab	Slash
Glide	Dab	Press	Float
Slash	Wring	Flick	Thrust
Dab	Glide	Thrust	Flick
Wring	Slash	Float	Press
Flick	Float	Slash	Dab
Press	Thrust	Glide	Wring

Less Gradual Changes Involving Two Elements

	Weight – Time	*Time – Space*	*Space – Weight*
Float	Slash	Dab	Press
Thrust	Glide	Wring	Flick
Glide	Thrust	Flick	Wring
Slash	Float	Press	Dab
Dab	Press	Float	Slash
Wring	Flick	Thrust	Glide
Flick	Wring	Glide	Thrust
Press	Dab	Slash	Float

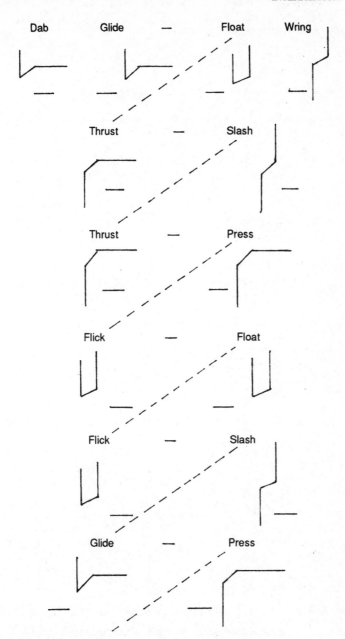

Dab Glide — Float Wring

Thrust — Slash

Thrust — Press

Flick — Float

Flick — Slash

Glide — Press

95

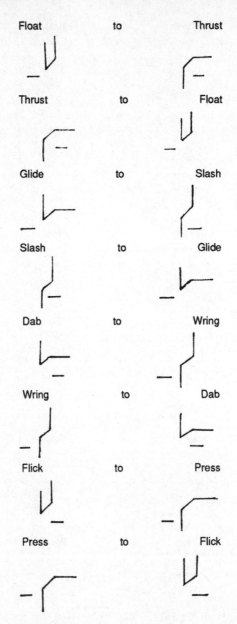

Float   to   Thrust

Thrust   to   Float

Glide   to   Slash

Slash   to   Glide

Dab   to   Wring

Wring   to   Dab

Flick   to   Press

Press   to   Flick

Abrupt Changes involving All Three Elements

Dynamic Action

Remember, an action will always be coloured by its accompanying emotional content. For example, many people returning home from work may open their front doors with a pressing/gliding effort and have no other concern than to turn on the light switch. They will effect a general harmonic pathway conforming to the structure of their body and the location of door knob and light switch. They are unlikely to try and accomplish the task by spinning around, lying on their backs and using the big toe of their left foot in a wringing/slashing effort! More than likely, the spatial pathway will originate from close to body centre, move forward on opening the door and move over to right high as they feel for the switch.

There are, however, individual harmonies resulting from physiological and psychological states. A dwarf reaching for the light switch, may need to exert greater than average effort as he strains upwards. He might need to jump quite high to reach the switch. A distressed person may be so upset that the simple action of opening the door becomes clumsy and ineffectual, the result of an inappropriate choice of effort action due to an emotionally confused state. A third person may take it all in her stride, meeting with no problems and expecting none.

We all tend to be selective in our movement behaviour. If the above characters were replaced by a trio having similar physiological and psychological states, it is unlikely that they would display identical movement pathways. Ideally, a healthy person should be able to encompass the whole range of human movement with ease. Only then can he select the movements most suited to his own nature in relation to the job to be done. Light and graceful movement may suit one person and be quite wrong for another whose personality is better expressed in rather jerky movements. This behaviour should be the result of choice on their part and not an expression of other mental, physical or emotional limitations.

Reminder

How long is it since you carried out any observation tasks? Return to your markets, factories, garden centres, offices, shops, cafes and crowded streets. Use your newly acquired knowledge. Try and recognise basic efforts, the transitions and the rhythmical sequences, especially those arising from repetitive work. Become proficient in this simple notation, using it as a shorthand. Read it back in the studio and try and recapture the actions you saw, including any expressive gestures.

Chapter 12

*Sound and Gesture Accompanying
the Eight Basic Effort Actions*

Sounds accompanying working actions are the audible result of an inner mood. Strenuous physical activity such as logging or hauling nets is usually accompanied by sound. We are getting used to tennis players accompanying their efforts with sound at Wimbledon. Extreme emotions such as great sadness or joy normally give rise to sound. When they don't, it often seems to us that another emotion, equally powerful, is holding the sound in check – perhaps a need to suppress the grief or laughter through fear or social obligation?

Let us take a simple approach. Try saying the words 'Yes' and 'No' with thrusting. The voice will be strong, sudden and direct. It may be directed at a real person or an imaginary one. It may, or may not, be accompanied by a thrusting gesture or a thrusting action. Whatever the bodily movements, the meaning will be quite clear. Here is someone who has made up their mind and is quite emphatic about their decision. It seems they will brook no argument.

Try a similar exercise with floating. Could you honestly say that this person appears just as emphatic? Does the essence of floating lend itself to such clear and unequivocal decisions? Is there not an element of doubt, of having not quite come to a solution; perhaps not even wanting to arrive at an answer.

Experiment with all the basic actions in turn, referring to our earlier notes if necessary.

Improvisation
Bear in mind, performers should keep to the designated basic actions, arranged beforehand, and not lapse into their own preferences. Remember, you must learn to extend your range of movement. Use gestures where appropriate and plenty of action. In the first exercise, for instance, you could use the whole room.

Exercise 1

The following conversation is for two partners. Each should select one effort action to use throughout. Movement of the body and the voice should be simultaneous.

'There it is!'   'Where?'   'Over there!'   'I can't see it.'
'You're not looking.'   'Yes I am!'   'Oh well, now it's gone.'
'Gone where?'   'Just gone.'   'Gone? Oh, no.'

Go through all the eight actions singly. Ability to move well, both through bodily and vocal expression, leads to an enormous variety of interpretations of this rather banal conversation.

Exercise 2

'Hi! I'm glad to . . . oh, it's you!'
'Yes. It's me. . . Look, let's. . . '.
'Alright. . . when?'
'Now . . I think.'

Try the above improvisation with each performer using two basic effort actions throughout. Having selected them, does it mean a gradual transition, a less gradual or an abrupt change? Work out the transitions carefully.

Repeat the exercise using different basic actions and the appropriate transitions. Where more than one transition is feasible, try them all. Don't forget to write your effort symbols down.

Exercise 3

The class stands in a ring facing the centre, with the right arm and leg behind the body. The weight is central in this open stance and the right fist is clenched. An imaginary punch-bag hangs in the centre of the circle.

On the command 'And', the circle thrusts forward with the right arm and leg, making an 'Aahh!' sound. The right leg takes the weight as it arrives in the forward position whilst the clenched fist halts at the invisible punch-bag. The exercise needs to be repeated several times with both sides. When the movement is successful and truthful in its thrust, the voice comes over well. It is useful also to attempt this exercise with the group closing its eyes whilst listening to named colleagues individually trying out the task. (If you need anonymity, number off!) It is quite clear to the listeners which performers are better at thrusting than others and this is borne out when they open their eyes and observe the accompanying bodily movement.

Exercise 4

Again the class stands in a circle – feet slightly apart with the weight more on the left side than the right. Imagine you have an ironing board in front of you. The left hand rests lightly on the imaginary board as the right hand glides horizontally across it to the right whilst the voice simultaneously makes an 'Aahh' sound once again. (The weight is transferred through stance to the right side.) Repeat several times on both sides. Remember, voice and movement should start and continue together throughout the exercise. (If you run out of breath, stop the movement. Try again.)

Try the exercise again with the group closing its eyes, as it listens to individual voices. Selecting privately what they think to be a true glide (or a very poor one), they should then open their eyes and see if their opinion is matched by the bodily demonstration. It should be.

Exercise 5

i). Try Exercise 3 with a thrusting movement of the body and a simultaneous vocal gliding of the voice.

ii) Try Exercise 4 with a Gliding movement of the body and a simultaneous vocal thrusting of the voice. I doubt whether anyone managed this successfully. It seems virtually impossible to produce a sound using one basic effort action and a bodily movement simultaneously using another. Even with highly trained artists, one can detect slight 'impurities' in the basic effort actions. There is a feeling of something being 'not quite right'. More of that later.

What is quite clear, however, is that sounds and words are the result of movements of the speech organs and share the same roots as movements of the body. Separately, or together, they are expressive of a mood.

If you wish to start with gibberish in the following improvisations, do so, but eventually progress to speech. These scenes are not meant to be naturalistic.

Exercise 6

Scene: Office. Table, two chairs.

An employer interviews an applicant for a position as secretary.
    The employer may only use a thrusting action throughout whilst the applicant must stay with floating. Keep the improvisation quite short; the ideas may be coming thick and

fast but it is hard to function for any length of time using only one basic effort action.

How did it go? Did you manage thrusting on every single word? Perhaps the employer's greatest difficulty was feeling that he had to wait for an answer from the applicant. It is better not to wait unless you keep your rhythm going with sounds, gestures and/or general movement, in this case, thrusting. If thrusting does not come easily to you when playing the employer you may well find yourself influenced by the gentler floating rhythm of the applicant. If this influence continues, you will no longer be thrusting but will find yourself in a transitional state and not nearly so emphatic. After all, the change from float to thrust is abrupt!

The problem for the student playing the secretary is also one of keeping to the given floating action. You must on no account be influenced by the employer's behaviour. Neither must you look at the employer directly. Your eyes must also be indirect, never really focusing on anything. This is extremely difficult to do when someone is speaking to you. because the most natural response is to 'look them in the eye'. If you find it hard, try following the flight path of an imaginary bluebottle. More of this later. Let us suppose that the student who is playing the applicant really feels very at home with floating. It may be that the student can float rhythmically over a whole sequence of words. This does not allow a 'diffident' thruster much chance to get a thrust in! And it is very offputting not to be able to look someone in.the eye if you are trying to be direct.
The reverse could happen. The applicant could be caught up in the Thrusting rhythm of the employer.

Exercise 7
Try Exercise 6 with the employer floating and the applicant thrusting.

The scene should involve plenty of activity. Use the table and chairs rather as an assault course! There is no reason why the thruster should not stand on a chair or the table or even under the table occasionally to prove a point. The Floater could wind himself up in knots over, through, under and around the chairs or table.

Exercise 8

i) Scene: Woman requires gardener. Greenhouse. Imaginary shelves. Plants of all heights.

Lady dabs. Gardener presses. Remember to keep to your own basic action and try not to be influenced by your partner's rhythm. Both players will have directness in common, i.e. both will 'fight against' Space. But there the similarity ends. The gardener will also 'fight against' Weight, producing strong resistance but 'indulge in' Time i.e. sustain the action over a period of time. The woman will not only 'fight against' Space, she will also 'fight against' Time but 'indulge in' Weight, i.e. feel a certain light relaxation.

ii) Reverse the actions.

iii) and iv) Exchange characters and repeat.

Exercise 9

i) Scene: Green room. Waiting to audition. Two or more characters each with a different basic effort action.

Improvise a conversation, intermittently going through your lines. Are you auditioning for the same part? If so, and you have selected contrasting basic effort actions, the interpretation will be very different. Do remember that we are staying with one action only and therefore cannot possibly attempt a naturalistic scene. Even so, the results can be quite extraordinarily clear.

Change around. Attempt other basic effort actions.

All my regular dance students have had to take weekly Laban-based voice and acting classes. This was not an attempt to turn them into actors. On the contrary, over the years I discovered that many movement problems arising in the dance class could be overcome through liberation of the voice. The movement of all the students improved and I learnt later that many underlying emotional problems were eased or resolved. I had not really considered this aspect of my own work before, although I knew the earlier movement classes had given rise to a feeling of well-being for the majority of students.

Derivatives Arising from the Eight Basic Efforts

If you look back at the diagram at the beginning of Chapter 11, you will notice that each of the basic efforts is situated at the confluence of three equally stressed elements, i.e. Weight, Time and Space. However, it is quite normal during daily life to stress one element in particular. Take flicking as an example. We might want to accentuate the suddenness of the action more than its flexibility or lightness – to transform the flick into a jerk! To indicate this we stress the Time continuum by adding a dot.

The Laban chart opposite can be used as a general guideline. You will notice that the first example, 'thrust', only becomes a 'punch' when Space is stressed, i.e. directness. I have often used punch as synonymous with thrust. Work through these gradations yourself, using exercise and improvisation. Sometimes the differences may be slight but, make no mistake, there *are* differences.

I suggest you try out the following exercises with a partner or in small groups. This allows one person to perform the exercise whilst others observe the movements closely, notating them and comparing results afterwards. Some discussion may arise among the onlookers concerning the accuracy of the performance. This is excellent. It means that you are becoming aware of the infinite variety of movement possibilities. Problems should be solved through corrected movement demonstrations. Verbal opinions are not enough!

It is better not to develop entrenched views. A beginner, attempting the same exercise several times can, without realising it, make subtle changes in time and stress. Keep an open mind. This doesn't mean an empty one; it does mean being truly aware of all the nuances of effort.

Exercise 1
Stance. With right side leading into the following directions:

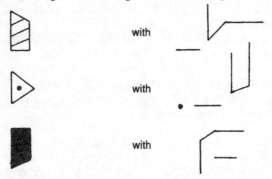

with

with

with

Repeat with the left side leading.

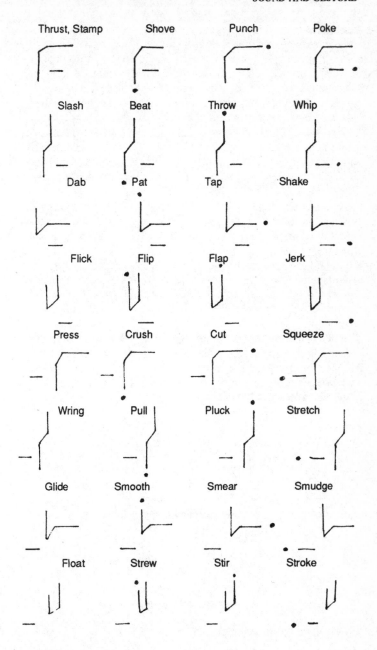

Exercise 2
Whole body moves freely:

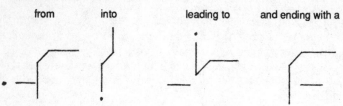

Exercise 3
Kneeling. Both arms leading the body.

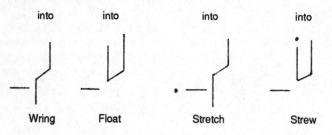

(Stretch is a derivative of Wring and Strew a derivative of Float).

Exercise 4
Show the difference between:

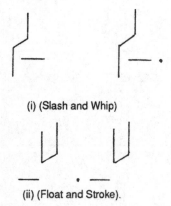

(i) (Slash and Whip)

(ii) (Float and Stroke).

iii) Try i) and ii) in reverse order.

Mobility and Attention to Detail

Don't get disheartened on your journey. Remember, we are trying to touch upon the whole range of human movement. No mean task! I have never met anyone yet who had such a wealth of expertise at their fingertips that they had no need to improve upon and extend their own range of movement. However, many colleagues have, with great success, used and developed Laban's theories in the course of their own specialised work; stimulating and inspiring others and the ripples from these sources have spread far and wide and continue to do so.

Further Exploration

You have so much information now that it is possible to create your own exercises. Give each other tasks. For example, study the actions of brushing your teeth, pouring coffee, cutting bread or dialling a telephone number or some other action you have to do in rehearsal. Write the effort symbols down. Perform the effort actions in front of a partner who will also write them down. Exchange notes and perform the action using each other's symbols. Do they agree? If not, why not? The basic efforts should be fairly easy to ascertain. The derivatives will certainly not be easy yet. Just keep practising.

Reminder

Go back to Chapter 3 and work through the Dimensional Scale.

Chapter 13

Time-Weight and the Greeks

The Greek Dance I learnt as a child had nothing in common with my subsequent research into its history. I was introduced to a two-dimensional style ('à la grecque') and exhorted to keep 'in opposition'. The 'frieze line', being the equivalent of the five positions of the feet in ballet, had obviously been lifted from the dancing figures appearing on Greek vases. These positions, performed in sequence along a straight line, represented an approximation of these illustrations.

My initial pleasure at temporarily getting away from ballet exams and the stress on 'turn-out', soon turned into disillusionment. Whilst I knew the origins of classical ballet, no one could tell me much about the origin of Greek dance. I soon suspected it was a 'phoney set-up'. Nevertheless, it was a great pleasure to be barefoot and wear a short, loose tunic and dance on lawns in the summer. I suppose we were pale reflections of Isadora Duncan.

I remember running in circles with neat little steps as fast as I could. 'Komats' were quite exciting. This was a step forward with one leg, a spring upward and forward with the other and, before the raised leg could reach the ground, the first leg overtook it and completed the landing. These steps could be performed in sequence or with intervening steps and hops travelling forwards or backwards. The only other step I recall is a leap off one leg, twirling round in the air, similar to a balletic attitude *en l'air*. I cannot remember its name. After being exhorted to keep to a straight frieze line or a perfect circular, two-dimensional formation even in komats, this sudden aberration into a wild, three-dimensional, bacchanalian movement scuppered me. At nine years, I decided that the teacher had got it wrong. The dancers on the vase did not truly represent Greek dance; the leaping, twirling 'attitude' was much more acceptable. I gave myself to it with abandon.

Many years passed before I realised how exciting Greek dances really were. I can only make a brief mention of them here.

Whilst we do not know the exact choreography of their dances (precise notation being unavailable), we do know they used rhythms to express emotional moods to accompany and enhance the drama. These moods covered the whole spectrum of human behaviour: drunkenness, despair, joy, rage, placidity, aggression, languor, solemnity, bawdiness, downright vulgarity and so on. As they mostly accompanied poetic or dramatic works, expression of deeply held emotions would require bodily movements capable of interpreting such feelings before an audience. (One should bear in mind the demands of the open-air amphitheatre and a vast audience.) In his book, *World History of the Dance*, Curt Sachs says:

So large a share in the drama could be possible only if the dance itself were possessed of dramatic potentialities. And this we know to be true from all the that the Greeks have written about their dances.

The Greeks believed that certain combinations of time units gave rise to definite expressive qualities. For instance, a short time unit followed by a long one seemed to them to give the impression of masculine energy. Its contrast was seen as expressing femininity.

In his book *Mastery of Movement*, Laban says:

In associating short and long duration with the weight-rhythm of accented and unaccented parts of a movement sequence, six fundamental rhythms have been found.

All other rhythms were considered to be variants of one of these basic rhythms. Rhythms or 'measures' (as in Shakespeare) were arranged in strophes to enhance the dramatic action. Laban gives the following chart, linking rhythm to significant mood:

THREE TIME UNITS

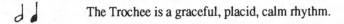 The Trochee is a graceful, placid, calm rhythm.

The Iambus is more aggressive and was, in spite of being used in the female Lydian mode, often taken as the male contrast to the Trochee. It is gay and energising without being rude and belligerent.

FOUR UNITS

The Dactylus is grave and serious, being used in procession on solemn occasions.

The Anapestus is a march rhythm indicating advance. It occurs in dances of moderate temper.

FIVE UNITS

The Peon is the expression of excitement and foolishness and, evokes alternately terrifying and pitiable states of mind. It appears in war dances.

SIX UNITS

The Ionian expresses violent agitation or its contrast, profound depression. The drunkenness of Dionysian festivals, languor and despair were expressed in this rhythm.

Two or more combined fundamental rhythms were associated with a mixture of moods:

a) Austere, belligerent, rude movements of masculine character. (The Dorian mood, using Dactylus, Anapestus and Peon).
b) Voluptuous, flowing, tender attitude of feminine character. (The Lydian mood, using the Trochee, Iambus and Anapestus).
c) Enthusiastic, religiously enhanced, passionate attitudes of a supernatural character. (The Phrygian mood, using the Ionian and Peon).

It seems that the Greeks already associated these moods with the Time-Weight elements of effort. (Long/short; accented/ unaccented). The same fundamental rhythms can be seen today and are especially noticeable when a repetitive working action is confined to one particular rhythm. If continued into leisure time, it could become a bad habit. (I am reminded of Charlie Chaplin's film *Modern Times*.) These were some of the problems confronting me when I introduced Laban's work into industry.

My twirling attitude *en l' air* must have had an Iambic rhythm!

110

For any actor-dancer, a study of the classical period of the Greek theatre in its heyday is essential to the serious student. It seems to me to encapsulate most of what we have been discussing in our own movement journeying. Perhaps the little information I offer here will whet your appetites for further research.

The early Greeks were of very mixed origins, all having their own dances and rituals. Despite regular wars between the many states, religious shrines and temples were held sacred by all parties and it is thought that this led, in later times, to uniting the populations everywhere in paying tribute to their gods at times of great joy and tragedy. Indeed, in some of the more remote mountainous regions, a few ancient rituals and dances have survived, coming down to us almost unchanged, although their meaning has been lost. Even the priests perform dance-like movements in their services and one is reminded of the leader of the chorus in Greek classical drama.

Like other cultures, the main themes dealt with birth, death, initiation, marriage and fertility. Festivals included solemn propitiation of the gods, joyous thanksgiving celebrations, drunken rites and mimetic, abstract and mystical dances. At all times, word and movement were inextricably linked and the songs were usually sung by the dancers themselves. As we have seen, the metres of the choral passages were specifically chosen to enhance the overall effect of the action. For instance, in the dionysian play, *The Bacchantes*, by Euripides, the rhythms are lively, exciting and swiftly changing, reflecting the hysteria and unrest of the dionysiac performers, who likened themselves to 'frisky colts'. Flutes accompanied Phrygian hand drums and shrieks!

Examples of Greek Dance
1. The word *choreia* (choral dance) was thought by the Greeks to come from chara, 'joy'. In Homer's *Iliad* (xviii), he describes the glory of the round dance as young men and women, especially chosen for their beauty, in superbly shining attire, opened the circle into lines running to meet each other, whilst in the middle two tumblers turned somersaults. A 'divine minstrel', the main dancer, leading with song and lyre.

2. Very little is known about the *emméleia* apart from the fact that it was a dance for women moving in closing and opening

111

positions and travelling in fluctuating circles around altars and shrines at times of religious ceremonials. References are made to its dignified and restrained character and its appearance in tragedy of the highest order.

3. The Macedonian *guerilla* folk dance of today probably had its origins in the pyrrhic, or fighting dance, of earlier times. It originated as a genuine preparation for fighting but was distinguished from a mere gymnastic exercise by artistic movement, rhythm and musical accompaniment. The dancers used the working actions of the soldiers, imitating the avoidance of missiles, throwing weapons, shooting arrows and striking blows with the arms and legs. Some of the most successful warriors in the field were also said to be the best pyrrhic dancers.

4. The *rhathapygízein* was a spectacular dance usually performed by young women and girls. One, or two feet, were simultaneously flung backwards to slap their posteriors energetically. Apparently, one young maiden so distinguished herself by accomplishing the feat no less than a thousand times without stopping that the poets of the day wrote verses in praise of her achievement.

5. Some dances stressed the throwing of the leg in a forward or backward direction whilst in others, the dancers sank to their knees and rose up again, simulating fertility.

6. In some of the tragedies of Aeschylus, a chorus of fifteen dancers entered five abreast and three deep; at other times, three abreast and five deep in the anapestic marching metre.

I have only given you a few brief examples of early Greek dance but I am sure you will have seen how they used the six fundamental directions in their dances, adapted working actions to dance rhythms and used a mixture of rhythms to express moods.

I am going to ask you to try out some exercises. Before you do, I would like you to take note of the following:

Symmetry is less passionate than asymmetry. It is used as expressive movement in enhancing the dignity of religious or ceremonial occasions. It has a stable foundation.

Asymmetry reveals excitement, a chaotic inner attitude in turmoil. There is a danger of losing control by exaggerating this imbalance, the result leading to irrational movements and gestures.

Be conscious of your floor patterns and also the pathways of your hands and arms. Are your turns closing inwards or opening outwards?

I have already reminded you of the six fundamental directions but don't forget the excitement of the pure diagonals and the relationship of the eight basic efforts.

Do you want your dancers to express one overall 'general' mood, i.e. solemnity or is there opportunity for individual behaviour to develop expressions of a more, perhaps, degenerate nature?

Exercises
i) I would like you to get into groups and experiment with percussion based on the given rhythms.
ii) Follow this with improvised group movement.
iii) Link the rhythms with the moods.
iv) Speak, intone, sing as you will.

Improvisation
Choose a solemn or a joyful occasion and choreograph your first attempt at a Greek chorus.

Reminder
In *World History of the Dance*, Curt Sachs discusses the work of Greek sculptors in portraying the characteristics of a choral dance: 'The observer admires the joyous rhythm which binds together, into a harmony more than personal, movements that arise from an inner compulsion and accord with the law of the dancer's own body.' Surely this is art of movement?

Chapter 14

Mental Effort Preceding Action

Sometimes actors and dancers seem to move 'perfectly', but without motivation. This has led to a misunderstanding of the word 'technique', which many people believe has nothing to do with the expression of feeling. On the contrary, for performers, technique is the ability to use the thought and feeling preceding an action, with awareness.

It is possible to link this mental effort with the motion factors of Space, Weight, Time and Flow. The following four phases of attention, intention, decision and precision may appear simultaneously or in any order or one or more may be omitted.

Space can be related to attention and the need to orientate ourselves satisfactorily to whatever focal point attracts us. We can accomplish this in an immediate, direct way or in a circum-spect, flexible manner.

Weight can be related to intention and the wish to do something may be firm and powerful or slight and gentle. How determined are we to carry out the action?

Time can be related to decision. Decisions can be made unexpectedly and suddenly, exchanging one thing for another as in 'a sudden change of mind', or they can be arrived at over a period of time, sustaining some of the previous conditions.

Flow can be related to precision or progression. We are able to control the natural flux of our actions by using bound or free flow, i.e. we can regulate the flux of our movement.

Example

A clerk's attention is attracted to a visitor entering his office. He reaches out to shake his hand just as the telephone rings. His intention to shake hands is cut short and he lowers his hand, his attention now directed to the telephone. He has a strong determination to answer it and reaches out just as it stops ringing. Once more he drops his hand, his intention again abandoned before carrying out the action. He could now return his attention to the visitor and his earlier intention to shake hands can go ahead, providing there are no more interruptions! The mental effort in each case is visible by small, expressive, bodily movements.

The phase of decision began already when the clerk lowered his hand in the first instance and there was a further example of decision when he again dropped his hand to answer the telephone. The completion of the actions did not materialise in either case. Decisions can either come about gradually, in a sustained manner ('lowers') or in a contrasting, sudden ('drops') manner.

The phase of precision occurs at the final anticipatory moment before performing the deed; it can be wary in an unfamiliar situation, resulting in a highly controlled effort due to bound flow. The opposite situation would lead to unconstrained effort due to free flow.

I have found this breakdown of the four phases of mental effort, prior to physical action, very helpful in observation classes. The student learns to associate the physical action with feeling and motivation. The movements of turning over a page in a book may seem identical when demonstrated by two people. But, if one is trained to look beyond the obvious, to become aware of small muscular tensions, one begins to gain an insight into the attitude of the person performing the action. In this example they could be very different.

Commonsense tells us that in everyday life, not all our gestures are conscious. Consideration of unconscious gestures or shadow movements is part of an actor's training in observation. They can precede or accompany an action, forming part of the individual's natural, characteristic effort make-up; scratching oneself, pulling an ear, rubbing one's nose, twirling a lock of hair and so on. Such gestures which appear to have no practical significance and lack purpose do, however, reveal an inner attitude which often highlights what is significant in a person's behaviour. A sensitive actor will, from time to time, consciously select such a gesture to enhance his role. On the other hand, through close identification with the character he is playing, he might use one of them unconsciously as a 'subjective' gesture.

There are also those everyday gestures which replace words, such as 'over here!,' 'there,' 'yes,' 'no' with nodding, pointing, winking, shaking the head. These are called conventional gestures.

Both unconscious and conventional gestures tend towards incomplete effort except under conditions of extreme excitement.

Take the shadow movement of gently coiling the index finger around a strand of hair. Lightness and flexibility are the two main elements. The unconscious gesture indulges in Weight and Space. Time is of little consequence. Under great agitation, the shadow movement could become a basic effort action with the addition of Time. It is possible, of course, that the attitude to Space and Weight will also change.

Imagine carrying an antique vase into a showroom. The owner of this treasure is busy talking to a customer and points to a space on a shelf, a conventional gesture. It could be an incomplete effort consisting of directness and slowness; indulgent in Time and resisting Space. Suddenly you trip over the antique carpet and part company with the vase. I imagine a full-blown basic effort action would materialise immediately! Later we shall see how to enhance our emotional responses.

I find it interesting that Stanislavsky believed that man's activity was composed of moments of attention followed by intervals of rest and reflection. He thought that attention on anything needed time before it turned into thought and could be expressed in words and action. There is a regular rhythmic pattern to this process in most people but somebody who is mentally unbalanced may display a broken rhythm of attention, the periods of rest appearing not to exist for him. He says such a person shows: *attention, attention and again attention. . . . words pour out of his mouth without conveying any meaning to normal people. The speech of a madman is just a dance of thoughts without rhythm or control. He explodes in a series of disconnected thoughts. . . .*

Stanislavsky found an analogy between attention and breathing, both being rhythmically linked. The healthy and composed person breathes through the nose in a rhythmically constant manner. This allows the body state to carry out its functions of renewal and regeneration in harmony. At times of emotional trauma, breathing becomes accelerated and uncontrolled. The breath comes through the mouth and creates more disequilibrium. Actors must learn therefore to control their respiration.

I believe that Stanislavsky's 'rest and reflection' are what Laban named intention, decision and progression. Certainly, abrupt changes of 'attention only' result in staccato-like movements and speech if there is any.

We have seen that bodily position is the result of previous movements which have themselves arisen out of our earlier, inner struggles. These positions can also foreshadow future activity by implanting anticipatory imprints on the body. We put ourselves in the right position to accomplish whatever is next expected.

Improvisation
This chapter lends itself admirably to improvisational work. A few shared given circumstances such as being greeted enthusiastically by a stranger, being accused of shoplifting or applying for promotion, can provide the basis for many different interpretations.

Reminder
Go into a café or a park and observe people on their own. Where is their attention? For instance, are they reading a book, looking at the other people around, feeding the ducks, staring into space, focused on their private thoughts, their shopping, the time or just dozing. Is their attention easily disturbed? Does his behaviour appear relaxed or are there tell-tale signs of tension? Do they appear indecisive? Do you notice any shadow movements? Is the warmth of a greeting belied by small movements suggesting an inner struggle to disguise feelings?

Chapter 15

Dance Drama

I am often depressed about the way dance teachers and choreographers approach dance drama as recreation rather than serious study. I also find it frustrating to see a director 'blocking' a crowd scene without being aware of the spatially exciting and expressively dynamic movement possibilities. For my part, I see no barriers between acting and dancing. Actors should be able to move naturally across into dance if required to do so. Dancers should be able to cross into acting, without fear of the spoken word.

Our actors, in the days of Theatre Workshop, could do this well. Some of them were far better modern dancers than those appearing with professional companies. Others were good movers, using their skill to enhance their characters. I hope this chapter will encourage more directors and choreographers to be courageous and discard these artificial barriers.

The standard of movement training received by an actor can never be too high. Actors communicate with their audience by movement. Voice is an extension of that movement. Actors do not need more movement training at drama school. They need better planned movement training. Jazz dance, contemporary dance, aerobics or whatever else is used in a class warm-up, is not necessary for an actor's training. They will never improve understanding of movement behaviour. Keep them for leisure time and concentrate on Laban's principles of movement.

If dancers are attempting to portray characters in dance drama they must work perceptively on inner attitudes. These will be determined by their characters' 'given circumstances'.

What are Given Circumstances?

By given circumstances we mean time, place, characters, situation, decor, music, costumes and props etc. It is not necessary to use all these although it is true to say that they all form part of the given circumstances. If one changes only one of the given circumstances, the entire story is changed.

The dynamic common to all drama is conflict, sometimes seen in terms of conflict between protagonists, i.e. man and his fate (Greek tragedy) or man and society (social drama: Shaw, Ibsen etc). One of the functions of drama is to purge the emotions through pity and fear or through laughter and joy. It is obvious then that drama is largely occupied with the emotions.

Acting out the Emotions

We can only act out emotions if we formalise them into bodily clichés. Certain gestures have become associated with certain emotions and have become acting clichés. For example, there is the melodramatic villain rolling his eyes, twirling his moustache and leering to show everyone that he's up to no good. The audience responds by joining in the fun, booing and hissing. Because the actor is using well-worn movement clichés they will not take the situation seriously.

The Chinese Classical Opera company, for example, use their sleeve positions as symbols in a more formalised approach to emotion. The actor-dancers display a formidable range of emotions by a precise vocabulary of gesture.

Wherever there is an onlooker, drama or dance drama becomes a performance. The performer is no longer working alone once he is aware of that observer. And both performer and observer will usually share a cultural tradition which the performer is able to draw on.

Today's dance drama in the West will only work if it depicts events and resolves a situation. Something must happen. The dénouement will resolve something. Think of *West Side Story*.

Narrative line in our dance drama can be either 'forward moving', i.e. horizontal or 'upward moving', i.e. vertical. A horizontal development moves through the thesis or statement, to the antithesis or conflict and is finally resolved by the catharsis or the removal of the forces which create the situation. When the dance drama is horizontal in form, it deals with the emotions. We already know our inner feelings have to go through certain phases before we can take any concrete action unless of course, we are prepared to limit our movement to clichés.) The individual character must be carefully worked out in advance as

119

this will influence the performer's interpretation. The more clearly defined a given circumstance is, the more precise the preparatory work and this, in turn, leads to truer behaviour.

A vertical development creates the drama by expressing the inner conflict of a situation through juxtaposition and external designs. It deals not so much with the development of a situation as with contrasting styles, each of which is imbued with a special significance by the performers, for example: A dance of atomic fission, a highly successful piece of choreography I arranged for the actors in Theatre Workshop for the play *Uranium 235* by Ewan MacColl. Atomic fission can be explained in terms of mathematical formulae but these are only convenient symbols. However, as the dance and every other art form has its own symbols, it is possible to parallel the symbols of the scientist with the symbols of the dancer. A vertical development is normally intellectual in content, dealing with ideas rather than emotions.

Quite often, dance drama is not so much concerned with a story as with an incident. This may mean that the artists are not so much concerned with human relationships over a period of time, as with human reactions to an atmosphere or a specific locale.

What do people do in a certain atmosphere? How can you create this atmosphere and express it in your bodies? The first task is to find the ingredients, i.e. the given circumstances. What kind of a day is it? Supposing the locale is a railway station, is it a large inter-continental station with bustle and noise, nothing permanent, everyone moving, to find their platform, to buy papers, snatch a cup of tea, buy cigarettes, look at the timetable, find a porter, enquire where the taxis and buses are or the metro. A general picture provides the groundwork for the emergent characters. As Laban says: *An actor can represent character and circumstance if he knows enough about their inherent effort characteristics.* The dancer in the dance drama, like his fellow artist the actor, must obey the same rules.

Characterisation depends on clearly defined analysis of given circumstances. The choice of movement sequences would, at first, be intuitive. He would be unaware of the quality of the efforts involved but by a gradual process of elimination, he would eventually arrive at the right phases of mental effort to portray, accurately, his character's actions.

Chapter 16

Objective Function and Movement Sensation

It is obvious that our state of mind affects the manner in which we carry out any action. Two recognisable mental attitudes are at work here:

a) objective function in which we are thinking only of the task in hand, and

b) movement sensation in which the psychosomatic experience increases the expressiveness of a situation.

Although both are present at all times, one or the other may assume dominance. Let us clarify the roles played by these two components in each of the three continuums of Space, Time and Weight.

Space   i) The effort element 'direct' consists of a straight line in direction.

ii) The effort element 'flexible' consists of a wavy line in direction.

Time   i) The effort element 'sudden' consists of quick speed.

ii) The effort element 'sustained' consists of slow speed.

Weight   i) The effort element 'firm' consists of strong resistance to weight.

ii) The effort element 'fine touch' (or 'gentle') consists of weak resistance to weight.

Any operation which can be termed as an objective function i.e. thinking of nothing but the task in hand, can be objectively measurable. For instance, an athlete's speed can be correctly ascertained. The bullet, arrow and golf ball's velocity and direction can be determined and weightlifters can match their strength against the weights.

In the human psyche, however, there are also feelings which accompany efforts. It would be impossible to measure them objectively but they can be classified:

Space   i) The effort element 'direct' consists of a movement sensation of threadlike extent in space, or a feel of narrowness.

ii) The effort element 'flexible' consists of a movement sensation of pliant extent in space, or a feel of everywhereness.

Time   i) The effort element 'sudden' consists of a movement sensation of a short span of time, or a feel of momentariness.

ii) The effort element 'sustained' consists of a long span of time, or a feel of endlessness.

Weight   i) The effort element 'firm' consists of a movement sensation of heaviness, or a feel of weightiness.

ii) The effort element 'fine touch' consists of a movement sensation of lightness or a feel of weightlessness.

The weight-lifter or athlete may go through their routine training schedules, (in which their prowess is measured precisely by instruments), on automatic pilot. But in our lives, the movement sensation is expressive of emotion. It has its roots in psychosomatic experience. Our vocabulary must change slightly to accommodate these enhanced expressive qualities.

It is possible to order these eight basic movement sensations in a similar way to those of the eight basic actions. (See Chapter 11, The Dynamosphere, page 88.) I think the diagram below clearly indicates the new variation.

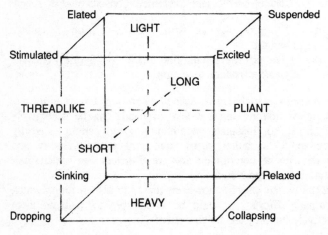

In Chapter 11, pages 86-98, I introduced you to tables showing the eight basic efforts. The accompanying movement sensations are listed below.

Basic Effort Actions

Movement sensation		*Objective Function*
Suspended Light-long-pliant		Floating Light-sustained-flexible
Dropping Heavy-short-threadlike		Thrusting Strong-sudden-direct
Elated Light-long-threadlike		Gliding Light-sustained-direct
Collapsing Heavy-short-pliant		Slashing Strong-sudden-flexible
Stimulated Light-short-threadlike		Dabbing Light-sudden-direct
Relaxed Heavy-long-pliant		Wringing Strong-sustained-flexible
Excited Light-short-pliant		Flicking Light-sudden-flexible
Sinking Heavy-long-threadlike		Pressing Strong-sustained-direct

123

Gradual Changes in Movement Sensation

Time		Weight	Space
Suspended	Excited	Relaxed	Elated
Dropping	Sinking	Stimulated	Collapsing
Elated	Stimulated	Sinking	Suspended
Collapsing	Relaxed	Excited	Dropping
Stimulated	Elated	Dropping	Excited
Relaxed	Collapsing	Suspended	Sinking
Excited	Suspended	Collapsing	Stimulated
Sinking	Dropping	Elated	Relaxed

Changes Involving Two Elements.

Suspended	Collapsing	Stimulated	Sinking
Dropping	Elated	Relaxed	Excited
Elated	Dropping	Excited	Relaxed
Collapsing	Suspended	Sinking	Stimulate
Stimulated	Sinking	Suspended	Collapsing
Relaxed	Excited	Dropping	Elated
Excited	Relaxed	Elated	Dropping
Sinking	Stimulated	Collapsing	Suspende

Abrupt Changes in Movement Sensations
Involving all Three Elements

Suspended / Dropping	Stimulated / Relaxed
Dropping / Suspended	Relaxed / Stimulated
Elated / Collapsing	Excited / Sinking
Collapsing / Elated	Sinking / Excited

Example

One of the more memorable trips in my early days as Laban's assistant took me to the Herefordshire countryside where I had been asked to lecture to the Land Army. In those days, I travelled with a croquet mallet for demonstration purposes rather than the more lethal axe!

The landgirls were friendly, but initially sceptical. By the time they had all tried out the various labour-saving exercises (with and without the mallet), I had won them over completely. Flushed with success, I showed them how to lift an imaginary weight without strain and then asked for volunteers to hold the mallet down, whilst I attempted to lift it against resistance.

A hush fell over my audience and all eyes focused on a girl sitting in the front row. She was about six foot tall and very powerfully built. Taking her time, she slowly rose to her feet and lumbered over to me taking the mallet silently with outstretched arms. The confrontation began to resemble the contest between David and Goliath.

With a bright smile and supreme faith in miracles and my training, I grasped hold of the mallet in the middle, bent my knees and tried to manoeuvre myself underneath it. I started to heave. Nothing happened. I continued to heave and edge my way underneath. Now, with better leverage, it started to rise slowly until I held the mallet triumphantly above my head. My opponent was gracious in defeat, crushing my hand in congratulations.

I mention this episode only to emphasise that my opponent was using great strength against resistance. She was certainly fighting against my attempt to raise the mallet.

Now let us take an imaginary situation which I'm sure many of you will have experienced at some time. It is the morning after a great celebration. You are not at your best. In fact, your whole body feels leaden as you attempt to go about your normal routine tasks. The movement feeling is one of weariness.

In both cases, we are discussing strong resistance to Weight. In one situation it was functional action against a real weight, or resistance, and 'strong' was the appropriate word. The movement sensation was only an accompanying factor. In the second, the movement sensation is prominent owing to the expressive situation arising from psychosomatic experience. We feel a sensation of 'heaviness' or 'weightiness'.

Imagine you have to push a heavy object through an open door straight ahead of you. We know that in using a pressing effort, we are resisting Weight and Space so that our movement is strong and direct. Time is a different matter. Here we are yielding to, or indulging in, Time by sustaining it. We have no great feelings about this functional action and, therefore, movement sensation is secondary, an acompaniment only.

Perhaps today you feel a little off-colour and everything needs extra effort. The Weight sensation in pursuing the object could again become heavy. The Time sensation could change to 'long' and the Space sensation to 'threadlike' or 'narrowness', if we are to stay within the pressing effort. We have now moved from functional action to movement sensation. Our feelings are no longer secondary in carrying out the task and our movement sensation is one of 'sinking'.

Of course, we could start with a pressing, functional action and suddenly believe ourselves to be overworked and 'ill done by', taking responsibility for someone else's job. The action could become heavy in Weight sensation, short in Time sensation but pliant (or crumpled) in Space sensation. This result has become slashing in a more expressive situation i.e. 'collapsing'.

We could try the above task in a very lighthearted manner, without much consideration for results. Let us try flicking. The flexibility, suddenness and lightness of flicking could become pliant, short and light, resulting in a movement sensation we call 'excited'. I doubt if the object will ever get far and certainly not through the open door!

Do bear in mind that I am isolating movements to explain the language. In real life, these movements will be accompanied by conventional or unconscious (subjective) gestures, transitions, incomplete efforts and drives.

Looking back over my contest with the landgirl, it is possible to see moments when my actions lost their objective function and psychosomatic experience coloured my behaviour. For a while my actions were no longer 'objectively measurable'. On the contrary, my behaviour reflected a more intensely expressive mood as I battled to overcome my opponent. This was not a permanent situation (we are talking about fleeting moments) but the excitement surfaced from time to time. I think my protagonist treated the whole exercise as objective function. She seemed singularly matter-of-fact until the end of the contest.

Flow

So far, I have not mentioned the transformation of the motion factor Flow. I liken flow to a river of communication running in two directions, i.e. outwards to the periphery of our kinesphere and inwards to our centre. Through its coursing, we are able to establish a relationship with the world.

As with the other continuums, we know it has strongly contrasting opposites, from very free flow to very bound flow. In terms of natural flux, we experience a going on or complete stoppage.

When considering the movement sensation of flow, we are concerned with fluency. Laban likened it to the movement of a fluid substance. The sensation of flowing on can diminish to pausing. In this case, although we are now still, the feel is one of a 'withheld' continuation, and is very different from experiencing a complete stop: .

Flow i) The effort element 'free' consists of unhampered flow.
ii) The effort element 'bound' consists of hampered flow or a readiness to stop.

Movement Sensation
Fluency i) The effort element of 'free' consists of the movement sensation of 'fluid' or 'flowing on'.
ii) The effort element of 'bound' consists of the movement sensation of 'pausing'. Although, in this case, the body may be still, the feel is one of 'withheld' continuation.

Mobility and Attention to Detail
Continue to work through the eight basic efforts. They are the foundation for your work as a performer. It may be that you have problems in sudden or strong or flexible movements. A slashing action will then present difficulties. Daily practice is the only solution, unless you are happy to be type-cast and inherit a role where the character also has difficulty in slashing!

Further Exploration
Try experimenting with an action which has a mental attitude of objective function. Keep to one or two basic efforts. Imagine a given circumstance which will change this mental attitude to one of movement sensation. Your behaviour will now be more expressive. You may, or may not, change the basic efforts but discover what happens to the three elements Weight, Time and Space.

Reminder
Do not be mesmerised by the vocabulary. We are attempting to find words in this chapter which accurately convey our expressive feelings. It is not easy because there are far more movements than there are words to describe them. Even so, the task is not impossible, as many actors have discovered.

Chapter 17

Incomplete Effort

Actions can occur in which two motion factors are stressed, one of which may be flow. We call such transitionary moments, incomplete elemental actions. They arise regularly in everyday situations and the most noticeable quality is that there is no particular attitude towards the time factor. Such incomplete actions tend to be of a casual nature, sandwiched between two basic actions. (I find beginners, initially, ·like to refer to the earlier list, or the effort cube diagram, for one-element transitions.)

Example 1
Imagine a speaker toying nervously with his papers, or gently touching his forehead, perhaps using a gliding-floating incomplete elemental action.

Example 2
Imagine an operator trying to place a plank of wood into a small space in the centre of a pile of such planks. He is using press-thrust as an incomplete elemental action. Pressing develops into press-thrust quite naturally as he completes the task. Strength and directness are maintained but a casual attitude has developed in the Time factor, the action being no longer sudden nor sustained. There is no great urgency to speed up the process because of an immediate lunch-break, nor is he growing tired or frustrated with the tricky task. The transition was of a casual nature.

Example 3
Such incomplete elemental actions can often accompany speech, showing themselves in small gestures. A person answering with, 'If you like', could possibly accompany the remark with a dab-glide of the hand. Someone calling out, 'You certainly won't!', would most likely accompany the remark with a thrust-slash! (Always remember these are transitions between basic actions.)

Try accompanying, 'If you like', with a thrust-slash and 'You certainly won't!' with a dab-glide. First of all, it is very difficult to do. One tends to speak with the same effort that one is using in the accompanying bodily movement. This contrast also makes the pronouncement comical and gives rise to confusion resulting from conflicting messages being transmitted.

In both incomplete effort actions and in drives (which I shall mention later), inner attitudes play an important role, heightening the mood which is translated into more expressive movement behaviour. For the performer, an understanding of incomplete efforts is essential. Inner attitudes can be deliberate or subconscious, as we have already mentioned. They can also be significant or functional.

Laban distinguished these inner attitudes as representing three pairs of opposites:

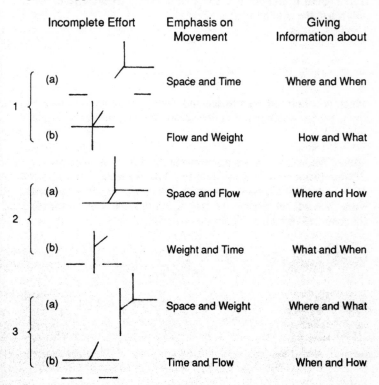

Incomplete Effort		Emphasis on Movement	Giving Information about
1	(a)	Space and Time	Where and When
	(b)	Flow and Weight	How and What
2	(a)	Space and Flow	Where and How
	(b)	Weight and Time	What and When
3	(a)	Space and Weight	Where and What
	(b)	Time and Flow	When and How

129

Our movement vocabulary now alters to accommodate each mood change and its characteristics. However, don't be thrown by this; Laban attempted to find suitably expressive words to match exactly the bodily actions arising from these inner attitudes. So far, no one has improved on them! Your job is to work on the movement experience and through it, discover the underlying mood for yourself. The motion factors of Space, Time, Weight and Flow do not change in essence but where each element was once regarded purely as objective, it is now coloured by inner participation. Understanding will come from working through the contrasting effort pairs. Take the first element of a pair, then the other and finally, both together. Work through all three pairs in this manner.

Example 1
1a) I think it helps to have a concrete situation in mind. Imagine reaching out in front of you and take hold of a friend's hand. We will relate the action to 1a)

which is concerned with Space and Time, giving us information about Where and When. Let us explore the possibilities of Space first.

Space. We know that our pathway can be direct (as an arrow) or flexible (wandering and smelling the flowers on the way). Space deals with the inner participation of Attention; we are concerned with 'Where' in Space. Is our focus on the object (hand) concentrated or embracing in orientation?

Exercise 1a
i) Focus on the object concentratedly.
(ii) Regard it flexibly, with an 'embracing' focus.

Time. We know that Time can be sustained or sudden. It deals with the inner participation of Decision and is concerned with 'When' in Time. The desire to take hold of a friend's hand can be:

(iii) sudden.
(iv) gradual.

Space-Time. We are concerned with the 'Where' in Space and the 'When' in Time. Our inner participation is one of Attention and Decision:

(v)   Concentrated and sudden.
(vi)   Concentrated and gradual.
(vii) Embracing and sudden.
(viii) Embracing and gradual.

You will notice that I am now using words which are more emotive in an attempt to describe the behavioural attitudes accompanying the action. We are linking the action with awareness of inner participation.

Could Exercise 1a) (v) be considered a confident and friendly approach, i.e. immediately focusing on the hand and making a sudden, snap decision to go ahead and take hold of it?

What does the change of behaviour suggest when in (vi) your concentrated attention is accompanied by a cautious approach? Does it, perhaps, show rather more careful consideration or uncertainty?

In (vii) what does an embracing focus imply when coupled with a sudden decision? Could it be that although the decision shows a certainty of behaviour, the attention, being more embracing in its focus, is rather more uncertain? Does this show an ambivalent attitude to taking hold of a friend's hand?

Finally, in (viii) we have the same embracing focus but now the decision has only been arrived at gradually. It does seem that a person with this behaviour is making 'heavy weather' when considering shaking a friend's hand! Perhaps, there is far more going on than we realise. Or perhaps, this is a person who always thinks and moves slowly.

It would seem from the above exercises that there is a great deal of awareness in the individual's approach to the given task. Awareness can be certain or uncertain.

Laban suggested the characteristics of the incomplete effort Space-Time were representative of an AWAKE attitude.

Example 1b
Let us remain, throughout all three pairs of incomplete effort, with this simple action of reaching forward to hold a friend's hand. Relating the action to

emphasising Flow and Weight, will enable it to reflect information about How and What.

Flow. We know that flow can be free or bound. Flow also deals with the inner participation of Progression (Precision). 'How' is concerned with whether we relate to the action boldly (i.e. with bound flow, extremely concerned with one thing) or with diffusion (i.e. with free flow, spread over and relating to the object freely, in very general terms).

Exercise 1b
(i) Try preparing to reach out boldly, in a totally concerned manner
(ii) In a more general, diffused manner.

Weight. Weight deals with the inner participation of Intention. Being concerned with 'What', the desire to carry out the task can be exalted or gloomy.

(iii) One's intention is gloomy.
(iv) One's intention is exalted.

Flow-Weight is concerned with How and What and our inner participation is one of Progression and Intention. Try the given task with:

(v) Diffused and gloomy behaviour.
(vi) Diffused and exalted behaviour.
(vii) Bold and gloomy behaviour.
(viii) Bold and exalted behaviour.

Could (v) above be considered another confident approach to reaching out to take hold of a friend's hand as in Exercise 1a) (v) of Space-Time? Diffused and gloomy characteristics do not augur well for making contact.

Exercise 1b) (vi) with its diffused and exalted characteristics is not ideal behaviour either in this context. In fact, although all these last examples (v)-(viii) appear to be particularly expressive of emotion and feeling, this emotion is not directed towards a focal point. Indeed, there is a lack of awareness in the person carrying out the task. This could be due to lack of visual relationship between the mover and his acquaintance. Space is dormant and without it, his attention has no focal point.

Laban suggested the characteristics of the incomplete effort Flow-Weight (which is the opposite of Space-Time) were representative of a DREAMLIKE attitude.

Example 2a
We will now relate the action to

which is concerned with Space and Flow, giving us information about Where and How. Let us explore the possibilities of Space first.

Space. We know that Space deals with the inner participation of Attention. It may be concentrated or embracing. Now it is paired with Flow and the resulting focus seems to be on oneself or of a more general, universal attention.

(i) Focus on oneself with regard to the action.
(ii) Your 'focus' is now outward and of a more universal attention. It can take in the hand of your friend but give it no more attention than anything else.

Flow. We know that Flow deals with the inner participation of Progression. It may be said to be diffused (free) or bold (bound). Now it is paired with Space and the resulting characteristics are either abandon or restraint.

(iii) Reach out with abandon.
(iv) Reach out with restraint.

Space and Flow are concerned with When and How and our inner participation is one of Attention and Progression. Try the given task with:

(v) Universal attention coupled with abandon.

(vi) Universal attention coupled with restraint.
(vii) Focus on self with abandon.
(viii) Focus on self with restraint.

I hope you haven't forgotten the original action was 'to reach out in front of you and take hold of a friend's hand'! It does seem that in the exercises (v) to (viii), there is little concern for the friend. The focus in his direction seems superficial at best, otherwise he tends to be ignored altogether. This behaviour, coupled with abandon or restraint, seems oddly detached in the given situation. In (v) and (vi) there seems to be a lack of commitment to carrying out the task. Perhaps other things are also seen to have equal, slight, generalised attention. In (vii) and (viii), it is obvious that one finds oneself more absorbing than any given task! Weight is dormant and, therefore, the more emotional quality (i.e. intention) associated with the element does not exist. Laban suggested the characteristics of the incomplete effort Space-Flow were representative of a REMOTE attitude.

Example 2b
We will now relate the action to

which is concerned with Weight and Time, giving us information about What and When.

Weight. Weight, as we know, deals with the inner participation of Intention. It can be strong or light. As no spatial quality is indicated in this incomplete effort, bodily actions will be particularly expressive of emotion and feeling. Therefore:

(i) your presence can express strong attachment.
(ii) or you can express a light, superficial touch.

Time. Deals with the inner participation of Decision and can be sustained or sudden. Influenced by the emotional quality of the Weight element:

(iii) your presence can have warm (sudden) impact.
(iv) or be careful (sustained) and considered.

Weight-Time. We are concerned with What and When. Our inner participation is one of Intention and Decision. Attempt the task:

(v) with a presence having (displaying) warm impact and expressing strong attachment.
(vi) with a presence having warm impact and expressing superficial touch.
(vii) with a presence having careful consideration and expressing strong attachment.
(viii) with a presence having careful consideration and expressing superficial touch.

Certainly, there is no 'remote' behaviour here. (v) seems a very warm and whole-hearted way of greeting a friend. Even (vi) could appear to be a genial, light-hearted, attitude. Perhaps (vii) expresses a more thoughtful, deeply felt, attitude. Does careful consideration and superficial touch mean that the mover has some doubts about the task or that he has other problems on his mind? In all the exercises, there is a feeling of personal, emotional, involvement.

Laban suggested that the characteristics of the incomplete effort Weight-Time were representative of a NEAR attitude. ('near' as in contrast to 'remote').

Example 3a
Let us explore the final pair of incomplete efforts. In

we are emphasising Space and Weight.

Space. We must remind ourselves once again, that Space deals with the inner participation of Attention, leading us directly, or flexibly, to 'Where' in our spatially orientated kinesphere. When the spatial element is emphasised in movement, shape becomes more clearly defined.

135

(i) The focus can be powerfully direct.
(ii) Delicately pin-pointing in a flexible manner.

Weight. Deals with the inner participation of Intention. The body sensation may be:

(iii) Strongly resolute, stubborn.
(iv) Lightly, sensitively, receptive.

Space-Weight. Concerned with Where and What, the inner participation is one of Attention and Intention. Try reaching out to take hold of your friend's hand:

(v) with a powerfully direct focus and expressing strongly resolute, stubborn characteristics.
(vi) with a powerfully direct focus accompanied by a light, sensitive, receptivity.
(vii) A focus which is flexible in its pin-pointing accompanied by strongly resolute, stubborn characteristics.
(viii) A focus, flexible in its pin-pointing accompanied by a light, sensitive receptivity.

In all the above exercises (v)-(viii), there appears to be a steadfastness of behaviour, a quality of reliability. In (v) the mover is powerfully focused, giving all his attention to the task with the greatest determination. In (vi) it could be that the mover is giving all his attention to the task with gentleness, understanding and receptivity. In (vii) the attention is flexible, darting, but there appears to be great determination to go ahead with the intention. Could one interpretation be that the mover is good-hearted but a little confused over the task? In (viii) there is a delicacy about these charactistics. A flexible focus accompanied by a sensitive, receptive, intention. The gentle intention may not be sufficiently strong to carry out the task when accompanied by a flexible, delicately pin-pointing attention. On the other hand, it could show great delicacy of feeling, a very gentle approach to the task. All the exercises show purpose , reliability and steadfastness.

Laban suggested the characteristics of the incomplete effort Space-Weight were representative of a STABLE attitude.

Example 3b
We will relate the action to

which is concerned with Time and Flow, giving us information about When and How.

Time. We know that Time can be sustained or sudden and deals with the inner participation of Decision. This decision to take hold of the friend's hand can be:

(i) slowly forthcoming.
(ii) sudden, abruptly changing.

Flow. Flow deals with the inner participation of Progression which can be free or bound. We can go about the task with:

(iii) Free, easy flow.
(iv) Bound, spasmodic (staccato) flow.

Time-Flow. Is concerned with When and How and our inner participation is one of Decision and Progression. It can be characterised by:

(v) A slowly, forthcoming decision accompanied by a lively, free, easy progression.
(vi) A slowly, forthcoming decision accompanied by a spasmodic, staccato-like progression.
(vii) A sudden, abruptly changing decision and a lively, easy, free progression.
(viii) A sudden, abruptly changing decision and spasmodic, staccato-like progression.

In Exercise (v) it has taken considerable time to reach a decision but once made, one feels its passage will be expedited by the lively, easy progression. The decision to reach out to a friend's hand has taken time but is followed through easily without any reservations. In (vi), the considerable time taken to reach a

137

decision is further hampered by a stop-start, staccato-like, progression. There is activity here but it seems to be of a cautious nature. In exercise (vii), the mover seems very excitable in his attitude. His abrupt changes of mind are accompanied by an easy, lively, progression. In the final exercise (viii), there is also a lively, excitable, attitude but the sudden changes of mind appear to affect the progression, creating a jerky, staccato-like, response. There is no concrete focal point. Perhaps the mover has too many things on his mind to carry out the task. The overall impression when trying out these exercises is one of adaptability, adjusting to situations.

Laban suggested the characteristics of the incomplete effort Time-Flow (which is the opposite of Space-Weight) were representative of a MOBILE attitude.

Mobility and Attention to Detail
It is essential to take time working through these exercises. Showing your work to other students can be productive, particularly if they are asked to guess the behavioural mode.

Further Exploration
Accompany your incomplete efforts with sounds, single words, short sentences. Do remember, voice is an extension of movement and should, therefore, arise naturally from the inner attitude, reflecting the incomplete efforts of the mode.

Reminder
Finally, try using the modes in other situations. If you work with a partner, you may well be using different modes. Experiment. freely but do not lose sight of the basic analysis of these expressive inner attitudes.

Chapter 18

The Four Drives

Drives combine three motion factors and are, therefore, more complicated than incomplete efforts. The qualities of the movements are highlighted, making them clear-cut in the case of purely functional movement and expressively enhanced in others, when Flow replaces one of the three basic factors.

Action Drive combines: Weight, Time, Space.
Vision Drive combines: Flow, Time, Space.
Spell Drive combines: Weight, Flow, Space
Passion Drive combines: Weight, Flow, Time.

Action Drive

We can relate basic effort actions to this drive, the combination of factors being Weight, Time and Space. Flow is latent. The quality of the movement, therefore, is one of objective function, i.e. a task carried out with no particular 'feelings' about doing it. (Even so, there is great aesthetic enjoyment to be gained from seeing a skilled manual worker doing his job with efficiency and expertise, using the right effort actions for the job.) Although in this drive the emphasis is on clear-cut action rather than emotion, movement sensation remains an accompanying factor.

I shall try to give you a 'pure' interpretation of each of the following three drives before discussing less dramatic examples.

Vision Drive

Vision Drive becomes 'vision-like' when Flow replaces Weight. Three variants from the incomplete effort chart (page 129) which do not feature Weight are the Awake (Space and Time), Remote (Space and Flow) and Mobile (Time and Flow) modes. You will remember we worked through each of these separately in the last chapter. When they synthesise, as they do in this drive, their effect on behaviour is far more pronounced than in the display of inner attitudes. I think I can best explain this through describing an imaginary situation and linking behaviour to some of the various characteristics found in the above modes.

Scene: A hostess is expecting a considerable number of guests to arrive. Indeed, some are already coming through the door. When they have all arrived, she has arranged to serve drinks. She is an experienced hostess and it shows in her easy, assured manner and cool, detached attention as she looks upon the general scene. Someone whispers that it is time to serve the drinks. At this moment, she suddenly cannot go through with her plan because she lacks the motivation to carry out her intention. She is incapable of making up her mind and is, therefore, quite powerless to act. She needs Weight to force her to do something. She is conscious of what is going on around her and is aware of her earlier decision to serve the drinks but can no longer go through with it. She is trapped in Vision Drive.

Any attempt to work with machinery would become a problem for the operator in this state. One fears for the ballerina about to leap into the arms of her partner as he momentarily goes into Vision Drive! Lacking intention, these two examples can be seen to be dangerous both to the machine operator himself and to the ballerina.

The basic effort action of flicking is, as you know, flexible in Space, light in Weight and sudden in Time. To transform it from the functional aspect to a more expressive display of feeling, we can introduce Flow as a replacement for one of the three constituents. Replacing Weight with Flow, we now have a vision-like flick consisting of sudden/free flow/flexible qualities, free flow having replaced lightness and gentle intention. It is possible to work through all the basic efforts in this manner.

Spell Drive

Spell Drive becomes 'spell-like' when Flow replaces Time. With the time quality virtually meaningless, the inner attitude is no longer concerned with sudden or sustained decisions. Three new variants from the incomplete effort chart which do not feature Time are the Dreamlike (Flow and Weight) Remote (Space and Flow) and Stable (Space and Weight) modes. When they synthesise, as they do in this drive, they again have a marked influence on behaviour. Here is another imaginary situation linking some of the characteristics found in the above modes.

Scene: An actor enters on stage. He starts off well and the audience is enjoying his performance. After a while, his attention becomes increasingly focused on himself and his intentions have become heavy and gloomy. He seems to be progressively restraining his delivery which has an air of detachment. Without the ability to make a decision, he cannot extricate himself from this situation.

Without the Time factor, he is out of kilter with everything around him, he has lost touch with reality. Fellow actors and audience alike have expectations which, in his present state, he cannot possibly fulfil. It is beyond his powers. He could giggle outrageously and be powerless to stop it. Wherever he fixes his attention, however powerful or exalted his intention and whatever flow he uses to carry out his role, without the Time factor he is, momentarily, suspended in a 'timeless zone'. There is an hypnotic feeling, a quality of 'fascination' as Laban calls it – rather like a small creature mesmerised by a boa constrictor.

Whereas in Vision Drive, the hostess could not go through with her plan because she lacked any kind of intention, the actor in Spell Drive has intention but lacks the ability to make any kind of decision which would result in releasing him from this emotional state.

I know very little about the stock market but I can imagine the disasters that could occur if those 'on the floor' went into a 'spell-like' drive and found it impossible to make decisions. Fortunes would be lost very quickly.

The basic effort action of gliding is, as you know, direct in Space, light in Weight and sustained in Time. Transforming it to a more expressive display of feeling, we will replace Time with Flow. We now have a spell-like gliding consisting of light/direct/free flow qualities. It is possible to work through the rest of the basic efforts in this manner.

Passion Drive
Passion Drive becomes 'passion-like' when Space (attention) is replaced by Flow. Three variants which do not feature Space from our incomplete effort chart are the Dreamlike (Flow and

Weight) Near (Weight and Time) and Mobile (Time and Flow) modes. When they synthesise, as they do in this drive, we have a strongly emotional behaviour pattern.

Scene: The Royal Festival Hall. You have gone there to hear the London Symphony orchestra play Mahler's First Symphony. For sometime you have given the music your undivided attention, listening intently and with pleasure. Gradually a change has come over you. Your pleasure has raised your emotional level to one of exaltation. This feeling has so filled your whole body that attention to anything or anyone has disappeared. The orchestra and the music no longer matter, It is as if the emotion has taken over completely. When this feeling leaves you, as it must, it is possible that you could well go to the other extreme and be 'bathed in gloom'!

Without the Space factor, there is no consciousness of shape. As there is neither direct nor flexible attention and therefore, no focal point, spatial clarity is missing resulting in stronger body sensation.

A choreographer, preparing a new work with a group of dancers, would have problems if one of the company lost his attention completely. A feeling for Space and shape would disappear and could well make difficulties for the other dancers, especially since he would tend to concentrate more on himself and his own feelings and emotions.

The basic effort action of floating is indirect/light/sustained. Transformed into a more expressive display of feeling, we will replace Space with Flow. We now have free flow/light/sustained which gives us a passion-like floating effort. Again, it is possible to work through all the basic efforts in this manner.

Well, that is the end of our own movement journey. It is a small part of the whole journey which is still going on. Laban's concepts remain immensely exciting, not least because they affect all of mankind. For my part, after fifty years I am still learning, still excited by all the possibilities, still exploring and testing my own ideas and developing them. I hope I have been able to pass on some of my own enthusiasm and that you will be motivated to continue the journey by yourselves.

Chapter 19

Steps

Many of my acting students have confessed to a horror of 'steps' when it comes to learning dance routines. The girls seem to have less trouble, probably because of dance classes in childhood.

Well, if you find yourself on 'the wrong leg' and happen to be standing on the right leg at the time, you know 'the correct leg' must be the left! But how is it that you seem to follow the instructions to the letter and still arrive on the 'wrong' leg? I would hazard a simple guess that it has to do with not knowing where to put your weight. As you will now see, this is very easily overcome. Pavanes, minuets, waltzes, polkas, tap routines and tangos are all within reach.

The notation in this chapter keeps to the symbols already introduced and remains very basic throughout, dealing only with direction and level.

The signs on the right side of the 'stave' denote movements of the right foot and signs on the left side denote movements of the left foot. Please note that it should be read from the bottom of the page upwards.

What is a step? A step is a transference of weight from one foot to the other:

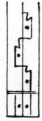

The right foot steps forward.

The left foot steps forward.

The right foot steps forward.

We start with our feet together in stance.

We need not necessarily travel in the forward dimension:

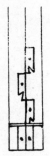

As the previous exercise but we are travelling backwards with backward steps. Make sure you transfer the weight with each completed step.

Stance.

Moving sideways to the right.   Moving sideways to the left.

You will notice that in both these examples, the steps alternate between open and crossed positions of the legs. This means that if you are taking a step to the right with the right leg, it will move to an open position. Stepping with the left leg over to the right, means it has to cross over the right leg, thus making for a crossed position. The opposite is also true.

We can also step backward or forward with a bias to the right or left:

Left-back with the left leg.

Right-back with the right leg.

Left-forward with the left leg.

Right-forward with the right leg.

Stance.

We need some lively music now with a regular beat. See if you can manage to read the following exercises:

Exercise A **Exercise B** **Exercise C**

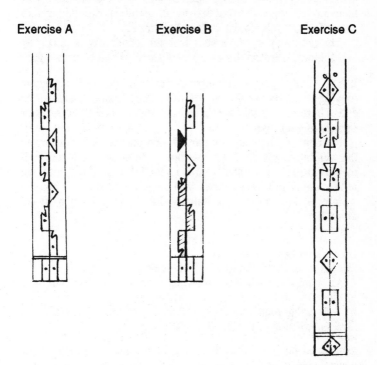

How did it go?

Exercise A
was fairly easy: stance, right step forward, left step forward, right step opening to the right, left step backward, right step crossing to the left, left step forward, right step forward.

Exercise B
I introduced a change of level. Stance, left step backward-high(demi-pointe), right step forward-high, left step forward-high, right step medium-right, left crossing step deep-right, right step medium-forward.

145

Exercise C
was a test of your ingenuity and my attempt not to add to our notational symbols! Stance started with feet astride. Both feet then moved together, returned to an astride position, together again, forward, backward and finally astride.

The only way to move your feet simultaneously is to spring. So each movement in this exercise is accompanied by a spring.

It is possible to perform all three exercises in sequence. If you are moving to a count of 4, you will have three 'spare' counts at the end. These can be taken as a rest or you can add three steps or springs of your own.

Remember, steps are not hard. It is a question of transferring the weight completely from one foot to the other. For instance, if the weight has been transferred from the left foot to the right, the left foot may still have contact with the ground but it will bear no weight. If this worries you initially, lift the foot slightly off the ground.

Half-Steps and Whole Steps
Simple to understand and a logical break-down.
i) Any single transference of weight which starts or ends in a closed position of the feet is a half-step.
ii) Any single transference of weight which starts and ends in an open position of the feet is a whole step.

In most of the exercises I have given you, stance has shown the feet together. (We could have started with an arabesque but that would have meant introducing more notation!). We, therefore, moved from a closed, to an open, position; in other words, taking a half step. This was followed by whole steps at various levels and in different directions.

N.B. Both whole and half steps mean a transference of weight.

What of Exercise C? Well, we did not actually transfer weight from one foot to the other. We remained with our weight centrally and evenly distributed throughout the sequence. We did not take half or whole steps. Instead we jumped with both feet simultaneously into various directions.

Try an improvisation containing a variety of half and whole steps. You can work on your own or with a partner and then demonstrate your routine to the class. It helps if you can teach and learn from each other. Joining some together tests the memory and can give you added confidence. You will probably work through the movements initially with bound flow. It takes time to learn, stop and put right and so on. But once you are confident, I would ask you to dance through the routine with panache and free flow, exuding confidence and enjoyment.

Variations
i) If it has all become too easy, accompany yourself with clapping or syncopate the rhythm.
ii) Try a routine followed by a quarter turn to face another part of the room, which now becomes the front. Repeat the sequence in this new direction.
iii) The above exercises can become very complicated if the basic routine already includes a part-turn.
iv) Try a half, three-quarter or a whole turn before repeating the routine.

What is a Gesture?
A gesture is a movement in any direction, at any level which does not take weight. In this chapter we are specifically concerned with gestures of the legs.

A deep level gesture lies just off the floor, a medium level would be approximately knee-high and anything above that would be considered high level.

When taking a half or whole step forward, the foot is lifted off the ground, the leg describing an arc as it travels forward through space to return to the ground and take over the body's weight once again. The movement after relinquishing weight and prior to resuming it, is called a gesture. So, every half and whole step is accompanied by a gesture.

In caricature or dance, gestures may be ornate, serving no real purpose as would be expected in Action Drive. For example, before stepping forward, the 'gesture' leg could explore sideways to high right, then to medium backward, followed by left sideways deep and proceeding finally to the transference of weight in the forward position.

Further Exploration
If you have assimilated all the above, try the following:

To a count of 4, make up a very simple routine of sixteen half or whole steps. On the counts of 5, 9 and 13, you must step into a new direction.

For the first four counts you will face the way you are going, For counts 5 – 8 inclusive, you will look to the right whatever direction your legs have taken! For counts 9-12 you will look upwards and for counts 13-16 you will look to the left. And the whole thing starts again!

We had a lot of fun in Theatre Workshop with these exercises and the company became so adept in their 'performances' that I added another hazard:

As before but on counts 1-4 hold both arms above your head, on counts 5-8 your right arm will be held out to the left, on counts 9-12 your right arm will be held forward and your left arm held in a backward position, on the final counts 13-16 your right arm will cross to the left and your left arm will cross to the right!

Do remember that once learnt, the attitude should be one of confidence in your ability to demonstrate the routine correctly and I would like you to use free flow on this occasion.

A shuffle in tap does not lead to an exchange of weight. Therefore, the shuffle is a gesture 'scuffing' the floor. What is a waltz but a half step followed by a whole step followed by another half step initially?

Take your time over this chapter. It should be fun to do and caters for the beginner and the 'expert'. Don't be afraid to improvise routines for yourself and others.

Chapter 20

In Search of the Character

You have been given your part and have read the play. How do you now go about using your knowledge of movement? Where do you start? How best to use the effort combinations to make the character come alive?

I will try and answer these questions by referring to a Theatre Workshop production of Federico Garcia Lorca's play, *The Love of Don Perlimplin and Belisa in the Garden*. My analysis of the play must, of necessity, be brief.

Lorca's tragi-comedy concerns an ageing, aristocratic, ex-Army officer, Perlimplin, who is being prevailed upon by an old family retainer, Marcolfa, to marry a young girl, Belisa. His initial reluctance to marry is transformed into passionate love for his young bride. Unfortunately Perlimplin is impotent and in order to fulfil Belisa's romantically passionate dreams, he creates for her an imaginary lover (The Young Man in the Red Cape). Perlimplin manages to maintain this fiction by disguising himself and serenading Belisa from afar, allowing her glimpses of the young man. Eventually, a confrontation is inevitable and Perlimplin kills himself.

Fantasy and reality are juxtaposed in the play and are transmuted into conflict of the flesh and the spirit. The themes of barrenness and impotence are present as they are in nearly all Lorca's plays. Another important dramatic element is the religious one, displaying Lorca's love-hate relationship with the Church. The play is also full of echoes of Catholicism. These motifs appear and disappear, co-exist and interweave, sometimes bold, sometimes tenuous throughout the play.

Don Perlimplin. Perlimplin is fifty years of age. The title of Don avows that he belongs to the aristocratic caste and, in the special conditions prevailing in eighteenth century Spain, would have meant that he had served as an officer in the Army. He has lived as a recluse for some time, sharing a large house with an old family retainer, Marcolfa. He is content to live in a world of books. Apart from Marcolfa, he appears utterly lost when dealing with human relationships. On his wedding night he falls back on a stilted mode of address typical of literature of an earlier period.

Driven into a situation with which he cannot cope, he takes refuge in fantasy. He appears to have spent most of his time indoors prior to marrying Belisa. When he creates the fantasy figure of the 'young man in the red cape', he appears to be part of the outside world; in reality, he does not leave his garden.

In Act 1, he wears a green cassock, a somewhat monkish habit. In scene iii, he wears the red cape of the young man; a symbol of the bull-fighter, of manliness, virility and youth. It might be said that he becomes a completely different character when he assumes the red cape.

Movement Analysis

The actor will, of course, have extended his own range of movement through regular vocal and physical effort training and freed himself from any 'personal movement habits'. He must also acquire some knowledge of the manners of the time.

Perlimplin, the scholar, has withdrawn from all human contact except Marcolfa's. He is a recluse who enjoys reading his books and is not called upon to make decisions. This leisurely life would be mirrored in his speech and movement efforts. He is unlikely to use quick and strong efforts. His walk would probably be slow (indulgent/yielding to Time), with stooped shoulders, the result of poring over books.

Perlimplin's inner peace is destroyed by Marcolfa's insistence on his marriage and, as a result, his normal effort patterns will be seriously dislocated. The actor is faced with the task of combining efforts which reflect Perlimplin's basic character on the one hand, with the efforts which show his increasing disturbance and confusion on the other.

It could be that as the recluse, Perlimplin can function 'objectively', i.e. selecting, reading and replacing his books in their right place. In his well-ordered life, he would probably be conditioned to arrive for his meals and retire at night at certain set times. A routine would have been established over many years. All that changes when he marries a young bride and falls passionately in love. As his confusion grows, the movement sensations which, before, were only an accompaniment to his functional actions, could now take over. They become more dominant in an expressive situation where psychosomatic experience is of paramount importance.

The actor could use shadow movements to precede, accompany or follow the character's functional efforts. Or he could stay with the 'intentional' mode, giving up and aborting the effort before having to carry through with a decision. He could consider moments or situations in which he could use incomplete effort combinations and/or Passion, Vision or Spell Drives. Slight, nervous movements of the hands or eyes could develop into a less economic and unco-ordinated use of Space when for, example, Perlimplin is wearing unaccustomed finery or confronting Belisa in the bedroom.

On the other hand, the actor may wish, at these moments, to show Perlimplin taking refuge in the formalised behavioural pattern imposed by traditional social mores. In this case, his nervousness would express itself through an exaggerated display of ritual behaviour. (This might, or might not, be accompanied by shadow moves.)

Obviously, the specific response to these situations would depend upon the total production and the relationship of one character with another, but whichever way the production went, a careful and exact working out of efforts would be vital.

Perlimplin's references to his childhood could be expressed as pleasurable experiences, in which he momentarily 'opens up', his voice and gestures becoming lighter and quicker in contrast to the slow-moving withdrawn recluse we see at the start of the play.

The gradual ascendancy of the 'young man in the red cape' poses one of the actor's biggest challenges. How does he determine this in terms of movement effort?

a) He might ask himself whether Perlimplin's imposture as the 'young man in the red cape' is meant to convince the audience from the beginning or whether the two are quite separate and Perlimplin the recluse is always visible in his movement characteristics within the young man.
b) At what point in the script does Perlimplin's identification with the 'young man in the red cape' become complete and, at this moment, are his movements those of a young man?

In view of the foregoing, it is imperative that once the role has been clearly defined in the production, the actor should be given opportunities to work on movement exercises calculated to develop these specific efforts. This includes improvisational work.

Commedia dell'Arte

A very popular play, *The Flying Doctor*, remained in our repertoire for nearly twenty years. It was an adaptation by Ewan MacColl of Molière's *Le Médicin malgré lui*, with notes by Biancolelli, an actor with the Commedia dell'Arte.

Briefly, the story concerns Gorgibus, the father of the inamorata, Lucille, and his attempt to marry her off to an old, but wealthy, suitor. In desperation, Lucille and her lover, Valère, decide on a plot to stop the proposed wedding. They persuade Sganarelle, Valère's valet, to disguise himself as a doctor who will advocate a change of scene and fresh air for the 'sick' Lucille. Gorgibus, ever gullible, agrees. The lovers are now able to meet undisturbed. The 'doctor's' disguise is discovered and Sganarelle is denounced as an impostor. As always, Sganarelle is able to wriggle out of his dilemma whilst assuring everyone that it has all turned out for the best.

Sganarelle. Sganarelle appears to be eternally youthful. He is an intriguer, a manipulator and a liar. He is a schemer whose plans often come adrift but his quick-witted behaviour tends to keep him one step ahead of trouble. More often than not, he turns the situation to his advantage.

He enjoys wine and is an inveterate flirt but careful never to get too involved with his paramours. Certainly, he never propositions women above his own station in life. He lines his pocket without shame on every possible occasion. This includes stealing which he will always justify on some pretext. In danger, he will take to his heels.

Self motivated, but never cruelly malicious, Sganarelle's humour, quick wits and ability to survive, have made him a popular rogue over the years.

Movement Analysis

Again, the actor must have extended his own movement range through regular vocal and physical effort training and freed himself from 'personal movement habits'. It is also necessary to acquire some knowledge of the characters of the Commedia dell'Arte, in particular of Sganarelle. Molière is believed to have taken Scaramouche as a model when playing the part of Sganarelle in *Le Cocu Imaginaire*. Certainly, our own Sganarelle had many of the qualities of this character.

Early movement rehearsals and improvisation can be based on what we know of Sganarelle's effort behaviour from our research and from the first play-readings. He is youthful, quick-witted and energetic; he will dart and flit about the stage. His thieving suggests sleight of hand and his playing on sympathy suggests a character able to express a variety of moods at will. We know he is a physical coward.

It is obvious from the above that the actor playing Sganarelle must be light and quick on his feet. He must be dexterous in his movements, able to run, changing direction and mood at a moment's notice. His hand gestures will be delicate and expressive as a dancer's.

Whilst all these qualities are inherently part of the character, they still provide us with only an outline, although an important one. We need to be more specific. Does this character never use strong efforts, never the occasional thrust or wring? Does his dabbing remain dabbing or does it transmute to a tap or a shake or perhaps, a jerk and finally a flick? And if it does, what are the inner attitudes that affect the effort action? Is the character using the elements, Space, Time and Weight, for objective functioning – carrying a message, putting on a cloak and hat or climbing through a window? Perhaps, movement sensation assumes overall importance and we are made aware of increasingly expressive situations, displaying, for example, excited and/or stimulated movement qualities arising from psychosomatic experience.

Perhaps Sganarelle's behaviour demonstrates moments of incomplete elemental actions and small gestures accompany his remarks, adding specific meaning and heightening a specific situation.

We could hypothesize for ever. What we need to do now is to go from the general outline to specific behaviour and this can only be achieved once the script has been studied in depth, the total production has been mapped out and the relationship between the characters understood. It is only then that we can select and refine the actions and reactions of the character.

Improvisational Exercise
Sganarelle, masquerading as the doctor, explains his methods thus:

I practice medicine for the pure love of it. I nurse, I purge, I sound, I operate, I saw, I snip, I slash, I split, I break, I tear, I cut and dislocate. I wage such cruel and relentless warfare against all forms of illness that when I see a disease getting the upper hand in a patient I even go so far as to kill the patient in order to relieve him of his disease, but I never make a mistake.

Work out your units and overall objective and once you know exactly how the speech should go, you have all the movement expertise to make it happen.

I worked on the speech with Howard Goorney and it became almost a dance. Yes, he did slash and thrust and even wring on occasion. He was lightly built, which was an asset, and had attended regular daily movement training over a long period. As a result, Howard was able to move flexibly and with ease, accompanying his speech with entrechats, spins, dropping suddenly to lying full length on his side whilst gazing up at Gorgibus and leaping up with a flicking action. One moment he was walking in assumed, deep contemplation, like Groucho Marx, and the next he was demonstrating his surgical 'skills' to all and sundry. That was our interpretation. You must work out your own character.

Reminder
Initially, the actor-dancer will have an intuitive approach to the role and will not consciously choose specific sequences of effort combinations. It is only when he gets 'into the part' and feels at one with the character that he can consciously select movement rhythms, spatial patterns and effort combinations, specifically 'honing' his interpretation of the character.

Postscript

Personal Views on Dance, Movement, and Acting

I have a dream that one day an actor may be required to dance and will think nothing of it. Just as a dancer will be called upon to carry out a speaking role and not be terrified of using her voice. They should be able to do both well; after all, the common denominator is movement. For a while, this choreographer and movement teacher worked in her own 'Utopia', Theatre Workshop. Although our own company finally broke up, its influence after some twenty odd years remains. Not only were we feted for our productions and dramatic skills, professional dancers such as Birgit Cullberg, choreographer to the Swedish Royal Ballet and Sigurd Leeder, dancer and co-founder of the Jooss Ballets, were fulsome in their praise of the actors' abilities to move.

A dance routine is, basically, just that! For example, the Bluebell Girls in Paris perform dance routines. They are not concerned with expressing individual character traits as they dance. Indeed, it would be an anathema in this context. In the American musical, *Chorus Line*, we saw trained dancers acting out their characters on stage. These performances, included solo dances which were expressive of emotional situations experienced by their own particular characters. However, at other times, the cast were called upon to dance literally as a 'chorus line', individual character being suppressed in favour of routine conformity, which we expect as part of the traditional musical.

In drama, actors are not usually expected to perform such 'dance routines'. The dance sequences arise from the play's action and the actors maintain their roles throughout. The waltz, mazurka, pavane or whatever, is an integral part of the play and the relationships already forged continue to interact throughout the dancing. The characters do not necessarily execute perfect steps in uniform precision.

The obviously skilled action of a chorus line routine may be pleasing and relaxing to the onlooker. It may be of a sufficiently high order to merit praise but is the audience moved, or changed in any way, by the experience? Does such a performance move the audience to laughter or tears, engage our sympathy or make us think? Only, perhaps, if someone were to fall behind in the music or use the wrong leg!

I am far more interested in the actor-dancer who has mastered the art of movement, using it through his stage character, to communicate to an audience, sometimes informing them and sometimes sharing with them, recognisable aspects of the human condition. It offers the audience a deeper experience of greater significance. We are made to think, we are emotionally involved as we witness how one fellow human being copes with life experiences. For a while, we are magically transported out of ourselves into a total experience which involves both the self and others.

Only a very few artists are able to evoke such responses. Even so, much more could be accomplished by today's students given the proper movement training.

Artificial barriers unnecessarily separate singing, dancing and acting. That is not to say that these disciplines do not still need some individual training but it should be remembered that they all spring from a common root, i.e. movement.

Example
The Ball given by the Capulets in Shakespeare's play, *Romeo and Juliet* should be specifically planned in terms of different combinations and sequences of efforts. As we know, these will arise from specific, ongoing actions and interactions. It is not enough to compromise by creating a generalised, harmonious, spatial pattern because rehearsal time is limited and the script is more important. It is like preferring to look at a poor repro-duction when you could have seen the original painting.

Over the years I have been privileged to teach on many dance courses. There is no doubt that everyone enjoys moving and there is great interest and excitement in the variety of classes offered.

In dance drama, teachers will frequently choose as their material scenes based on classical or mythological plots. For many reasons, these are a good choice and, indeed, Shakespeare also used them. They have been tried and tested and proved to be psychologically sound. The basic plot still has meaning for us to-day; we can still feel for Odysseus as he encounters and attempts to overcome one danger after another. Character and voice, on these courses, are not studied in depth. They do not feature prominently because the students are on a dance or movement course. The result is a generalisation of the scene. Whilst I do understand this experience may be an invaluable and refreshing experience to school teachers on vacation, it does not seem to me to lead anywhere; artistically, for instance, what happens next year? Is the student offered another 'generalised' experience and will it be quite so enjoyable? Some people may find this quite acceptable. It seems that myths and classical drama are, therefore, not only popular material and of value to the student of dance drama. They are, above all, safe material.

The influence of Laban during my training, followed by my years in Theatre Workshop and my own natural inclinations, have never led me to opt for 'artistic safety'. That is not to say I would never choose to base a choreography on an ancient myth. I think they are ideal for children and, perhaps, newcomers to movement and dance. (I spent many exciting weeks with twelve year olds improvising scenes from Odysseus).

But what lost opportunities for the more advanced students! Why not be more adventurous and topical; re-live the old myths, turning the situations to man and events of the twentieth century. Make statements about the human condition today; about those with power and those without, the group against the individual, the weak versus the strong. The list is endless. We live in extraordinary times. Let us experiment with contemporary themes and have the courage not always 'to play safe'.

I believe that it is up to the teacher of dance drama to open a door onto the world of character exploration. So, first of all, we must spend a little time on the script and on the relationship of the characters. In short, follow Chapter 20. This approach does not lessen the movement experience. Rather does it hone and formulate a character study, paring away the dross and unnecessary activity, until we are left with something truly exciting which will capture everyone's imagination. We have now moved from the 'general' to the 'specific'. The experience for the individual student could be profoundly moving and this will communicate itself to an audience. Even more importantly, he or she, will have taken the first step to becoming an actor-dancer.

Bibliography

Howard Goorney, *The Theatre Workshop Story* (Methuen).

Rudolf Laban, *Choreutics* (Macdonald and Evans).

Rudolf Laban, *The Mastery of Movement* (Macdonald and Evans).

Rudolf Laban, *A Life for Dance* (Macdonald and Evans).

Rudolf Laban, *Modern Educational Dance* (Macdonald and Evans).

Rudolf Laban and F. C. Lawrence, *Effort* (Macdonald and Evans).

Rudolf Laban, compiled by Lisa Ullman, *A Vision of Dynamic Space* (Falmer Press).

Lilian B. Lawler, *The Dance of the Ancient Greek Theatre* (University of Iowa Press).

Joan Lawson, *European Folk Dance* (Pitman and Sons).

Valerie Preston-Dunlop, *A Handbook for Dance in Education* (Macdonald and Evans).

Curt Sachs, *World History of the Dance* (Allen and Unwin).

Constantin Stanislavski, *Building a Character* (Reinhardt and Evans).

Constantin Stanislavski, *An Actor Prepares* (Methuen).

For information about practical workshops in Laban technique, please write to the author of this book:

Jean Newlove
c/o Nick Hern Books
14 Larden Road
London W3 7ST